BLUE GUIDE

KT-394-609

THE VENICE LIDO

A BLUE GUIDE TRAVEL MONOGRAPH

by
Robin Saikia

Somerset Books • London

Acknowledgements: Friends, colleagues and well-wishers have been enormously supportive throughout this project. They include Oleg de Baikoff, Charles Godfrey-Faussett, Thomas Howells, Geoffrey Humphries, Elisabeth Meinertzhagen, Charles Payne, Holly Snapp, Stephen Tucker and Joachim von Halasz. Special thanks are due to Hugo Vickers and John Julius Norwich, who were enormously generous with time, humour and anecdote. In Venice, thanks are due to Leone Jannuzzi and Salvatore Pisani at the Excelsior, Ester Trentin at the Golf Club, Aldo Izzo at the Jewish Cemetery, Eugenio Nardin at the Panorama Hotel and all the staff at the Hotel des Bains, the Tavernetta restaurant, the Lion's Bar, the Hotel Villa Mabapa, the Aeroclub Nicelli and Harry's Bar. I am indebted to Giorgio and Patrizia Pecorai, the father-and-daughter team responsible for the inspiring journals *Lido di Oggi, Lido di Allora*. I should mention my sons Inigo and Sebastian, committed Italophiles at a tender age and spirited sources of inspiration, and Alexander, who in common with Goethe first saw the sea from the Lido. I am indebted to my editor Annabel Barber, who repeatedly kindled and rekindled inspiration. Finally I thank my beloved Vicki, the most beautiful and clever companion anyone could wish to have on the warm and seductive shores of the Lido.

CONTENTS

PROLOGUE

This book is an unashamedly personal view of the Lido, coloured by my prejudices and enthusiasms. These were kindled when I first came here nearly thirty-five years ago, at the end of a school trip to Venice. We were staying at the Pensione Seguso on Zattere, then a fairly reserved establishment, a favoured retreat of James Lees-Milne. The trip was led by the genial and worldly Drawing Master at Winchester College, Grahame Drew. Everyone was to fly back to London except two of us, me and a friend, Oleg de Baikoff, I destined for Athens, he for Vienna. Grahame's kindly but firm parting shot was memorable. 'You've one more night at the Seguso. You'll be absolutely fine so long as you don't do three things. Avoid them with the ends of several barge poles. Don't go to Harry's Bar, don't drink grappa—and do *not* go to the Lido.' Later that night, after martinis at Harry's, we rolled along the Riva degli Schiavoni and caught the *vaporetto* to the Lido, clutching our bottles of grappa. We ended up in the brightest-looking bar on the Gran Viale with a gang of friendly young Italians who invited us to a party. We crammed ourselves into their dangerous Fiat and tore off towards the pine forest and beach at Alberoni. There we roasted fish on hot stones and drank wine until dawn, finally falling asleep amid the trees and dunes. I awoke in the blaze and breeze of mid-morning, stripped and flung myself into the warm shallows of the Adriatic where, in a specifically spiritual sense, I have remained ever since. This book is an attempt to communicate my boundless love for the Lido and to encourage all its readers to head for its warm and glamorous shores.

Robin Saikia
Hotel Excelsior, 2010

AH, THE LIDO! THE LIDO!

'Do any of you gentlemen know Venice!' suggested
Frangipane. 'For I should be delighted to reminisce
with him. Ah, the Lido! the Lido!'

Birds of a Feather, Marcel Nadaud

An important source of information about life in old
Venice is *Le arti che vanno per via nella città di Venezia*,
Gaetano Zompini's 1789 account of Venetian street
traders. Alongside the predictable assembly of knife-
sharpeners, candle-sellers and wig-makers are listed the
rather more unusual *castragatti*, the cat-neuterers. The
cat population of Venice had always been a problem and
Venetians were always ready to embrace a solution stop-
ping short of total massacre: cats kill rats, rats spread
plague, so neutering the toms would have seemed a
good way of keeping a useful ally under control. But
over time the feral population inevitably grew until it
was beyond the power of the *castragatti* or anyone else
to contain it. Visitors to Venice in recent decades will
remember the old ladies who fed the strays every morning along the Giardini Ex Reale. It was quite a sight.
Hundreds of cats would appear, from bushes, rooftops,
from behind pillars, leaping out of gondolas, snarling

at anyone who dared walk too near to the piles of fishy scraps dished out by the well-meaning crones. Tempers ran high on Rialto and soon the Comune di Venezia was forced to take action. The cats were exiled to the island of San Clemente, formerly the site of Venice's lunatic asylum for women, where they settled in well, their nocturnal mews harmonising neatly, some said, with the ghostly screeches of long-dead inmates. All seemed well until 2005, when the island was sold and redeveloped as a luxury hotel, the San Clemente Palace. The cats were again dispossessed. Again they were loaded into cages and cat-carriers and hoisted, mewing, hissing and spitting, onto a procession of barges. This time they were rehoused, despite much initial protest from the locals, at Malamocco on the Lido. Today the colony on Via Teodato Ipato, run by the dedicated cat charity Dingo, numbers upwards of 200, is growing by the month and looks set fair to stay.

It seems appropriate that the Lido[1] should once again be the refuge of exiles, for that was what it was at the very beginning of Venice's history. Malamocco, now a small and picturesque fishing village midway along the west coast of the Lido, was the ancient seat of government before its citizens consolidated themselves on

1   Purists say 'Lido' but 'the Lido' is acceptable and often used. It is pronounced *Lee*-do. On no account say *Lie*-do, the accepted pronunciation for Britain's outdoor swimming complexes. The following jingle may help: Your dog, *Fie*-do, loves the *Lie*-do! My dog, *Gwee*-do, loves the *Lee*-do!

Rialto, 'Rivo Alto', the 'high ground' upon which Venice proper now stands. The ten-mile-long sandbank now known as the Lido (from the Latin *litus*, meaning 'shore') was the site of the very first settlement of refugees from the Italian mainland, driven here by Attila the Hun and later by Charlemagne. From that original settlement Venice quickly grew—and though the early settlers eventually abandoned the Lido as Rialto expanded, it remained an important part of Venetian life and lore and was repeatedly acknowledged as such at home and abroad. In the Renaissance, envoys and ambassadors would deliver formal eulogies, praising a ruler and his family, celebrating the beauties and virtues of a principality and its people. Venice had more than its fair share of these and they were carefully noted, filed away, and from time to time published in collections. One of the more ingenious eulogies was delivered by the envoy Paolo Novello of Belluno in 1234. Novello adapted what was then a popular theme, the Seven Wonders of the World, outlining his own 'seven wonders' of Venice, among them the beautiful location, Venetian kindness and Venetian mercantile supremacy. His final 'wonder' was the Lido on account, he said, of the protection that it had afforded the Republic both from the sea and from her enemies. This was certainly true and would have been appreciatively noted by the doge and senate, for the Lido was indeed the beach and bastion of Venice, for centuries protecting the lagoon from the tides of the Adriatic and from succeeding waves of invaders.

Throughout the thousand-year history of the Venetian Republic, the Lido radiated potent symbolic importance as the outer boundary of Venice, consistently remaining a backdrop for ceremonial, a garrison for troops and a place of recreation. In the 19th century, after the fall of the Republic in 1797, with Venice under French and then Austrian rule, it found new life not only as a bathing resort but also as a place of striking natural beauty, praised by a succession of foreign visitors including Byron, Ruskin and Henry James. Later, after the unification of Italy, the development of the grand hotels and the inauguration of the Film Festival, the Lido became a glamorous international resort, rivalling the French Riviera. Today, after a new wave of regeneration, the beaches and hotels are as diverting as ever and the Lido remains an agreeable bolt-hole from the ever insistent and sometimes overwhelming beauties of Venice. The Film Festival is still a spectacular annual event; the grand hotels, the Excelsior and the Hotel des Bains, have reinvented themselves and kept pace with the times; the beaches have been immaculately spring-cleaned and now sport the all-important Blue Flag.

Yet despite all this, the Lido is unjustly and mysteriously neglected by travel writers and historians. If they mention it at all, it is often a mere curiosity, at best an unremarkable *bel niente* and at worst a somewhat vulgar beach playground with no intrinsic merit. And the detractors are by no means undistinguished. Israel Zangwill, in his *Italian Fantasies*, made the following decidedly uncharitable remarks: 'Even Goethe, it is amazing to discover from his *Italienische Reise*, never saw the sea till he went to Italy. And his first glimpse of it was, of all places in the world, at the Lido in Venice! He with the German Ocean to draw from him, as it drew from Heine, the cry of "Thalassa!"; he who might have seen how "Die weissen Meerkinder hoch aufspringen und jauchzen, übermutberauscht"[2], must fare forth to another land and behold a lazy, almost tideless lagoon lapping in shallow muddiness on the tamest and dullest shore in the world.' Later, in the hurly-burly of the 1920s, Robert Byron complained of 'water like hot saliva, cigar ends floating into one's mouth, and shoals of jelly fish'[3] And D.H. Lawrence, in *Lady Chatterley's Lover* (1928), offers a thoroughly damning description:

> The Lido, with its acres of sun-pinked or pyjamaed bodies, was like a strand with an endless heap of seals come up for mating. Too many people in the piazza, too many limbs and trunks of humanity on the Lido, too many gondolas, too many motor-launches, too

2   The quote is from Heine's *Die Nordsee*: 'The white foam-children spring aloft, mad with a fierce, exultant pride.'
3   In *The Road to Oxiana*.

many steamers, too many pigeons, too many ices, too many cocktails, too many menservants wanting tips, too many languages rattling, too much, too much sun, too much smell of Venice, too many cargoes of strawberries, too many silk shawls, too many huge, raw-beef slices of watermelon on stalls: too much enjoyment, altogether far too much enjoyment!

This book, which is built on the principle that there can never be too much enjoyment, attempts to set the record straight, focusing on the Lido's history and how it has inspired the succeeding generations of Venetians and tourists who have come to love it.

As Jan Morris wrote in *The World of Venice*, 'these reefs are places of drama and romance, soaked in history as well as sun-tan lotion, and still the sacred bulwarks of the Serenissima.' Lovers of the Lido will tell you that it can match Rialto, Venice 'proper', ghost for ghost, memory for memory, treasure for treasure, offering an infinite tableau of pleasing happenings, experiences and images: Isadora Duncan, photographed by her brother, dances ethereally along the sand on a rain-driven stretch of deserted beach; Coco Chanel perches piggyback on the shoulders of Serge Lifar in 1928, while in 2009, Karl Lagerfeld unveils Chanel's latest collection on a catwalk on the Excelsior beach; Byron gallops full tilt alone at dawn, from the desolate sands of Alberoni to the shaded cemetery at San Nicolò;

when Chateaubriand traces his name in the sand, the Adriatic rolls gently in to wash it away; Princess Jane di San Faustino, in flowing white robes, stands guard alone outside the doors of her beach hut, unsettling the passing *jeunesse dorée* with her 'basilisk stare'; an adventurous Lillie Langtry dives to the seabed, rising triumphant with an exquisite Persian jewel engraved with a love poem[4]; the barrel-shaped figure of Elsa Maxwell bobs determinedly across the floor at Chez Vous, the restaurant of the Excelsior, followed by her girlfriend Dickie Fellowes-Gordon; Diaghilev lies alone and dying in his darkened room in the Hotel des Bains, perhaps recalling the time when Stravinsky, at the ballroom piano, played him the 'Danse des Adolescentes' from *Sacre du Printemps*; the novelist and self-styled priest Frederick Rolfe, alias Baron Corvo, wanders alone, homeless

---

4   The *Nelson Evening Mail* of 15th June 1903 carries the following report. 'Most of our popular actresses, according to an article in the *Playgoer*, are partial to "mascots". Here is an inventory of the luck-bringers of five of the most prominent: Mrs Brown-Potter: a cats-eye ring and an emerald ring and emerald necklace worn on her birthday; Miss Violet Vanbrugh: a long chain of uncut turquoises, which she always wears on the stage; Mme Bernhardt: opals worn on her birthday, necklet of nuggets given her by the miners of California, a girdle of cameos; Mrs Langtry: a Persian turquoise, engraved on which is a Persian love-letter. Mrs Langtry fished it up while diving in the Lido at Venice.' This raises the interesting question, never satisfactorily answered, of the circumstances in which Lillie Langtry would have been diving off the Lido. Was she holidaying aboard James Gordon Bennett's yacht, *Namouna*? She is often identified as the seated figure at the right in the American Belle Epoque painter Julius LeBlanc Stewart's painting 'On the Yacht *Namouna*', Venice 1890 (in the Wadsworth Atheneum, Hartford, Connecticut).

and penniless, across the sands in the chilly March of 1910; thirty thousand Frankish crusaders, encamped here in the searing summer of 1202 at the outset of the Fourth Crusade, learn that they are finally to set sail and celebrate by fixing blazing torches to the tips of their lances so that it seems the whole Lido is ablaze; in the First World War, the poet-airman Gabriele d'Annunzio rallies the 87th Italian Air Squadron, 'La Serenissima'; the Duke of Windsor visits, in gilded youth and later in bitter-faced old age, Mrs Simpson at his side and, never far away, his long-suffering equerry, Fruity Metcalfe; Churchill is on the Excelsior beach with the inevitable cigar, huddled in an oversized dressing gown; and in 1911, in the Grand Hotel des Bains, Thomas Mann glimpses a striking young Polish boy, the inspiration for Tadzio in *Death in Venice*.

Today the Lido is no less colourful and alluring, in or out of season. Carpets of shells crunch underfoot; tractors arrive on the beach at dawn to clear away the seaweed and dead crabs; rollers follow them, smoothing the tousled coverlet of sand. Here are the boys who rent out pedalos and sailboards; there go the Dravidian kite-sellers and Nigerian handbag-merchants, patrolling hungrily back and forth along the beach. There are the bronzed lifeguards, the children leaping from piers and pontoons, the artists who colonise the *murazzi* (*see footnote overleaf*) with their ramshackle driftwood shelters. Away from the beach, along the Gran Viale and in the surrounding streets, there are the Liberty villas, their gates and façades alive with wrought-iron, stone or ceramic lions, lilies, nymphs, tritons, butterflies, dragonflies and spiders, their pilasters, ogee arches, gardens and statuary shaded by palms and cypresses. The *capanne*, the beach cabins of the Excelsior and the Hotel des Bains, are rented by Italian families who save up for this summer treat, for either the timber cabins favoured at the Excelsior or the straw-topped variety known at the Hotel des Bains as *tuculs*. There, glamorous old ladies, grandmothers the rest of the year but now self-appointed countesses or film stars for a week, play cards and drink *prosecco* under the candy-striped awnings. Out of season the hotels remove the straw tops from the *tuculs*, revealing the naked, skeletal frames beneath. Then, the beach at low tide, strewn with driftwood, is combed by families collecting *vongole* for lunch, clutching the distinctive bright yellow plastic bags of the local Billa supermarket. Flocks of goats invade the *murazzi*[5]; flounders are stranded in

5   The *murazzi* are the enormous spurs of Istrian stone that form a dam, protecting Lido from erosion by the Adriatic. The idea was conceived by a priest, Vincenzo Coronelli, in 1716 and developed further by the engineer Bernardo Zendrini. The project, completed in 1782, was an immense improvement on the make-do-and-mend *palade*, piles of rocks that had previously been dumped in the sea as a temporary measure. The *murazzi* were damaged first by storms in 1825 and later by the serious floods of 1966. Today, the *murazzi* are augmented by *pennelli*, piers comprised of boulders, jutting out into the sea at regular intervals along Lido's Adriatic seaboard. These double as anti-erosion measures and a convenient place for artists to build amusing shacks out of driftwood.

the shallows; dogs of all shapes and sizes leap and bark for joy along the endless, endless strand in the glassy February sunshine[6]. This is the Lido I love and that I invite the reader to share.

6   Dogs are a lively and attractive feature of Lido life. Alert Hemingway fans will remember a reference in one of his poems to 'Afdera's on the Lido'. He meant the private beach cabin of the Franchetti family, recalled by Baroness Afdera Franchetti in her charming autobiography, *Never Before Noon*. She describes a visit to the Lido long after the glory days described by Hemingway. It is out of season in February and deserted, but in a momentary reverie she half expects to see the ice-cream man she remembered from childhood, and the family bathing cabins, hers emblazoned with an 'F' for Franchetti and nearby the 'C' of the Cicognas. Presently the dream gives way to winter reality. There is nobody on the beach but a solitary man bent against the wind, walking his dog.

WE WED THEE, O SEA

When Jan Morris described the Lido and other lagoon reefs as the 'sacred' bulwarks of Venice, she had in mind the *sposalizio del mare*, the ceremonial marriage of the Doge of Venice to the sea. The ceremony took place at a strategic point off the northern tip of the Lido at the mouth of the lagoon. First celebrated on Ascension Day 1177, the 'marriage' marked Venice's support for Pope Alexander III during his struggle against the Emperor Frederick Barbarossa, whose territorial designs on northern Italy had caused considerable anxiety in Rome. As a symbol of his gratitude to Venice, the pope presented Doge Sebastiano Ziani with a ring and with it the right to 'wed' the sea. He stipulated that the doge was to cast the ring into the waters of the Adriatic, uttering the following unequivocal formula: '*Desponsamus te Mare, in signum veri perpetuique dominii*' (We wed thee, O Sea, as a sign of our true and perpetual dominion), a dramatic affirmation of Venetian supremacy rendered all the more potent by its having been bestowed on Venice by the pope. The ring was formally presented to the doge on Ascension Day after a ceremony in St Mark's at which Frederick Barbarossa, in a dramatic act of obeisance, kissed Alexander's feet. Ziani received other symbolic gifts from

Alexander III,[7] but the ring captured the popular imagination best since it was carefully calculated to recall Venice's hallowed treasure, the ring of its protector, St Mark the Evangelist.

It was no accident that Venice had chosen Ascension Day for the ceremony at San Marco and for the inauguration of the *sposalizio*. It was on Ascension Day 1000, nearly two centuries prior to the presentation of the Alexandrine Gifts, that Doge Pietro II Orseolo had set sail from the Lido on his triumphant expedition against the Dalmatian pirates. Ever since that campaign, there had been an annual thanksgiving ceremony at the Lido in which the Patriarch of Venice would offer the following prayer: '*Ut hoc mare nobis et omnibus in eo navigantibus tranquillum et quietum concedere digneris te rogamus, audi nos*' (Hear us as we worthily entreat Thee to grant that this sea be tranquil and quiet for our men and all others who sail upon it). The simple but powerful service also celebrated St Nicholas (San Nicolò), the patron saint of sailors and an increasingly popular figure with Venetians as their maritime empire flourished. The annual celebration was popular too, a firm bedrock on which

---

7   The so-called Alexandrine Gifts to Doge Sebastiano Ziani comprised two lead seals, a white candle, a sword, a parasol, eight ceremonial banners and eight silver trumpets. It is not within the scope of this monograph to investigate the symbolism attached to each of these, but a good game for clever older children at a loose end in Venice is to track down the many depictions of the Alexandrine Gifts, in pictures and statuary, to be found in the Doge's Palace, the Accademia and the Museo Correr.

to build an even richer ceremony centring on Pope Alexander's ring: the simple act of thanksgiving would be transformed into something infinitely more potent, a marriage. For marriage, like baptism, communion or any of the Seven Sacraments, is an outward sign of spiritual grace—a clear indication to her allies and enemies that Venice enjoyed God's blessing in all her enterprises. Given all this, it is no surprise that historians sometimes refer to the Lido as a 'metaphorical extension' of San Marco, referring to the way in which the *sposalizio* annually transmitted the sanctity of the basilica to the church of St Nicholas and the coastal waters of the Lido.

St Nicholas had long been loved by Venetians. Over time his cult was enhanced by ceremonial and his role in the hagiography of Venice became ever more sophisticated. He was the perfect gatekeeper at the threshold of the lagoon, ever watchful at his Lido vantage-point, assisting St Mark the Evangelist with the protection of the city. The dual importance of the Lido as home to his cult and as a sacred outpost of the basilica was finally set in stone by Doge Domenico I Contarini. A prolific builder of churches and monasteries, Contarini expanded and restored the basilica and in 1053 built the church of San Nicolò al Lido. Nevertheless, despite the physical presence of a church, and in time a monastery, on the Lido, a further obstacle to symbolic perfection had yet to be overcome. Venice, in common with all Catholic principalities large or small, took its patron saints seri-

ously. Saints fulfilled numerous roles, all of them of vital
importance in medieval Europe. They were, alternately,
badges of divine approval, objects of devotion, sources
of reassurance for simple folk, enhancers of civic pres-
tige, stimulators of trade and much more. Whatever role
a saint might be called upon to play, his cult would be
not be considered complete without a set of relics, the
more complete the better. This requirement may well
have been rooted in expediency or superstition or both,
but in time it was ratified by Pope Gregory the Great,
who stipulated that churches should only be founded
in places that could be proven to have a genuine connection to a saint.

In 828, according to Venetian lore, the remains of
St Mark had been rescued from Alexandria by two
Venetian merchants, Rustico da Torcello and Buono
da Malamocco, the latter, incidentally, a native of the
Lido. The enterprising pair are said to have smuggled
the Evangelist's remains out of the Saracen-held Muslim stronghold by hiding them in a consignment of
pork, a memorably picturesque claim that was also
entirely plausible, given the widely publicised unscru-
pulousness and ingenuity of Venetian traders. Further
strengthening the Evangelist's connection to Venice,
there was a no less picturesque tale of how St George, St
Nicholas and St Mark had been ferried to the mouth of
the storm-tossed lagoon by an old fisherman. There, in
Lido waters, they sank a supernatural ship, crewed by

devils and heading under full sail for Venice (the devils would have been equated in the popular mind with
one of Venice's ever-present enemies, the Dalmatian pirates). As a token of gratitude, the Evangelist presented
his ring to the old fisherman who in turn presented it to
the doge. There are several variations on the story, but
the general drift is always towards the idea that St Mark
and his ring are the exclusive property of Venice.

Whilst the cult of St Mark was firmly underpinned
by such relics and stories, Venice did not possess the
remains of St Nicholas, nor did there seem to be an easy
way of getting hold of them. They had been removed in
1087 from his birthplace, Myra, by the people of Bari
who claimed, with some justification, to have rescued
them from desecration by the Seljuk Turks, who had
recently overrun Asia Minor. However honourable this
Barian mission may have seemed to outsiders, Venice
and Bari were bitter mercantile rivals in the Adriatic and
it was therefore a source of considerable irritation to
Venetians that Bari should possess such a popular and
prestigious relic. Pilgrims—and their cash—descended
on Bari while Venice looked on disgruntled, its own
shrine to St Nicholas in danger of becoming nothing
more than a parochial curiosity, an ornamental venue
for inward-looking annual ceremonies. But then, at the
beginning of the 12th century, a miracle of sorts was
followed by a dramatic reversal of fortune for the saint's
Venetian cult.

In 1101, towards the end of the First Crusade, a Venetian naval contingent made a detour to Myra, where a detachment of sailors was sent to inspect what remained of the old church of St Nicholas. There, among the wreckage, they found a copper urn engraved, some say all too conveniently, with the words 'Here lies the Great Bishop Nicholas, Glorious on Land and Sea'. This they took back to Venice and, following their triumph, there has been to this day a lively debate as to who possesses the real relics of St Nicholas. As Professor Edward Muir of Princeton neatly puts it in *Civic Ritual in Renaissance Venice*, 'Saint Nicholas in the end divided his favor: Bari became the goal of pilgrims, but Venice captured the commerce.' While the coup at Myra undoubtedly strengthened the cult of St Nicholas, Venice's quest for relics was not quite over, since it still lacked the remains of its third patron saint, St George, the underwriter of the city's military, as opposed to its naval, endeavours. In 1462, the senate put out a call for relics, offering an open commission to any Venetian at large in the Adriatic to procure 'by prudent means and without violence' the widely mythologised but hitherto elusive head of St George. The head was found and brought to Venice where it remained in obscurity on the island of San Giorgio Maggiore until 1971, when it was rediscovered in a cupboard by the historian Kenneth M. Setton.

Following its inauguration, the *sposalizio* became increasingly dramatic over the centuries, providing an excellent opportunity for Venice to impress her foreign guests. In 1594 the English traveller Fynes Morison noted the doge's famous ceremonial barge: 'In the said compasse of the armory lies a great boat called "Il Bucentoro", because it corries [sic] about the number of two hundred; which boat hath upon it a kinde of chamber which useth to be richly hung, and covered over when in the same the duke and senators be carried by water at some times of solemnity, especially at the feast of the Ascension, when of an olde custome they goe forth to espouse the sea by the ceremony of flinging a ring into the same...'

There were three focal points in the ceremony: first the Basilica of San Marco, where Mass was sung; second, a specific point in the open sea, at the mouth of the lagoon by the Lido, where the ring was cast in; finally, San Nicolò al Lido, where the doge and his guests disembarked for prayers and an evening banquet. The two celebrants were the Patriarch, the spiritual guardian of Venice, and the doge, its temporal master. After Mass in the basilica, the doge set forth in the state barge, the *Bucintoro*, accompanied by Venetian magistrates and foreign ambassadors. The procession, as pictures by Canaletto and others reveal, was composed of any number of craft, all very elegantly decked out, belonging to the *Scuole Grandi* (the charitable organisations and guilds of Venice), the noble families, merchants, musicians and to a colourful and notorious sector of the Venetian community, the courtesans. There was an uproar in 1617 when the respectable women of Venice took exception to the increasingly brazen presence of the courtesans at the *sposalizio*. They successfully petitioned the senate to restrict the antics of the expensively dressed *poules de luxe* and the English ambassador, Sir Henry Wotton, reported that the festival 'hath been celebrated here with a very poor show of *gondole*, by reason of a decree in Senate against the courtesans, that none of them shall be rowed *con due remi* [with two oars, i.e. in a stylish boat more suited to a gentlewoman]; a decree made at the suit of all the gentlewomen, who were before indistinguishable from those baggages'.

As the *Bucintoro* approached the mouth of the lagoon and the threshold of the open sea, a more restrained flotilla could be seen making its way south from the cathedral of San Pietro in Castello. This was the patriarchal barge and its retinue. When it drew near, the barge would circle the *Bucintoro* as the head priest of San Marco, the *primicerio*, sprinkled the doge with holy water (*movens se cum navicula sua, quae ad latus dextrum steterat Bucentauri, circuit ipsam Ducalem, spargendo in D. Ducem, et omnes aquam benedictam*). Then, at a signal, the Patriarch would pour a vast pitcher (*mastellus*) of holy water into the sea, while the doge simultaneously cast in his ring.

Following this climax, the rest of the day was comparatively informal but nevertheless characterised by an unmistakable intermingling of sacred and secular symbolism. After Mass at the church of San Nicolò al Lido and a banquet, the first pilgrim and merchant ships of the season would leave for the East, blessed by the Patriarch, the morale of their crews uplifted by participation in the highest ceremony of the Venetian festive calendar. It may have been St Mark whom the sailors revered as the guardian of their city, but it was St Nicholas to whom they turned when they were afraid or homesick. And the spire of San Nicolò al Lido was their last sight of Venice on an outward-bound voyage, and the first on their earnestly prayed-for return.

COLONIES & CRUSADES

In the 1920s Mussolini instituted a regime of organised leisure known as *dopolavoro*, which means, literally, 'after work'. Throughout Italy the Fascist government built large and well equipped *colonie*, 'colonies', where whole families were encouraged to tackle bracing outdoor sports and other activities. Though the facilities on offer in the *colonie* were broadly popular in Italy, for years a stock threat volleyed at a naughty child would be: *ti mando a colonia!*—you're off to the colony—the threat of a spell of remedial 'exercise' usually serving to bring youngsters to heel. The *colonia* on the Lido, at Strada della Droma at Alberoni was as Spartan a bootcamp as any in Italy. True, the activities were not unremittingly focused on the hard cut and thrust of competitive physical games. In July 1936, for example, there was a genuinely edifying sandcastle competition held on the beaches of the Lido, where the children were asked to build replicas of their favourite buildings from the Roman Empire. After the prizegiving, a choir of local orphans sang the newly composed *Coro dei ginnasti* and the Lido Fire Brigade performed a gymnastic display, as did a specially trained team of deaf and dumb children from the Lido orphanage. But despite such diversions, the *dopolavoro* regime was challenging, one of Mussolini's many attempts to reincarnate ancient martial traditions, which in past centuries had been as much in evidence on the Lido as they had been elsewhere in Italy.

The Lido had, since early times, been a favoured location both for farming and military training, two activities impossible to promote in the cramped, residential confines of Rialto. As Venice grew as a naval power, it became increasingly important to ensure that in the event of war or invasion all able-bodied men should have at least some basic training in the martial arts. The open spaces of the Lido were ideally suited for this and by 1338 the civic registers note that over 30,000 Venetian men were capable of bearing arms, many of them accomplished crossbowmen. Regular exhibitions of various warlike disciplines were organised on the Lido for visiting dignitaries and the English ambassador Sir Dudley Carleton, Henry Wotton's predecessor, reports in 1609 that he had been invited to an exhibition of shooting with Turkish bows. He added that he was the first ambassador who had been asked to see this ceremony, though it is true to say that Spartan and Corinthian ideals had been promoted in Venice from the earliest days, celebrated in a kind of annual Venetian Olympics that took place on the beach:

From Doge Ziani's day [the 12th century] came the annual athletic festival on the Lido. Lads turned fifteen, and young men up to thirty, after careful training in their various *sestieri* or city wards, went off to the butts and tracks set up upon the beach to contest for prizes in shooting, wrestling, boxing, running, and other sports. The competitors were arranged in twelve groups called *Duodene*, and every one was expected to be a proficient bowman. Merchant ships always carried a certain number of such expert young bowmen. All 'catches' were permissible—indeed kicking, wringing the neck, and all the features, brutal as they were, of the Olympian grievous boxing were not disallowed. Bamboos as well as fists were used! All classes of the male folk of the islands were eligible to compete in every contest and upon equal terms. Matrons and maids thronged to watch and encourage sons and sweethearts, each fair one scrupulously careful about her dress and veil. Many a Venetian 'Venus de Milo' doubtless longed to try herself against her companions, but such maiden contests were inadmissible by the State laws.[8]

In the event of war, or preparation for war, the spacious wastes of the Lido were an ideal place to muster troops prior to embarkation. An added advantage was that during these preparations, Venice herself would be preserved from the squalor and disruption that in-

8   *The Dogaressas of Venice: The Wifes of the Doges* by Edgcumbe Staley, 1845.

evitably attend troop manoeuvres of this kind. In the later centuries of the Republic, when Venice employed foreign mercenaries in her Turkish wars, the Lido was an ideal place in which to segregate, drill and contain the frequently unruly and ferocious contingents of soldiers drawn from around Europe and the Mediterranean—Albanians, Dalmatians, Istrians, Prussians. But the first major mustering of foreign troops on the Lido, over 30,000 Frankish knights, took place much earlier, at the outset of the Fourth Crusade in 1202.

In the recent book *Great Cities of the World*, its editor, John Julius Norwich, contributes an essay on medieval Venice in which he attributes the city's early supremacy to three important factors. First, there is its impregnability: Venice's unique position protects it from invasion by land or sea. Second, there is the element of trust: a merchant nation that trades vigorously and widely and pays its bills on time will inevitably prosper. Last, there was the Fourth Crusade, an enterprise that enriched Venice considerably, leaving her in possession of 'a quarter and a half quarter of the Roman Empire', though the crusaders left a trail of carnage that blackened the name of Christianity for centuries to come.

The architects of the Fourth Crusade were the French noblemen Theobald of Champagne, Baldwin of Flanders and Louis, Count of Blois. Their plan, in response to Pope Innocent III's call to arms, was to attack Cairo, which by the end of the 12th century had become the principal powerbase of Islam. The aim was to topple Muslim supremacy in Egypt and thereby make the surrounding territories safe for European Christians to cross on pilgrimage to Jerusalem and the Holy Land. The attack would need to be by sea since Syria, the only gateway to Egypt by land, was already in Muslim hands. Who could help? It made sense to strike a deal with Venice, the strongest naval power in the Mediterranean and the only one capable of helping orchestrate an assault on this scale. Accordingly, envoys were despatched and an agreement was struck with the doge, Enrico Dandolo: in return for 85,000 marks and a share of any plunder or conquest, Venice would provide ships and active help to an international contingent of crusaders, mostly but not exclusively comprised of Frankish knights and their retainers.

The plan, ideal in theory, began to unravel when the crusaders assembled in Venice. To the dismay of their commander, Boniface of Montferrat, far fewer knights mustered than had originally been expected. Many simply dropped out, while others chose to make their way to Egypt under their own steam. As a result of the shortfall, the crusaders were unable to raise the agreed 85,000 marks, although after much drama—selling silver and gold plate, borrowing money at exorbitant rates from Venetian moneylenders—they did manage to raise nearly 50,000 marks. But this wasn't sufficient to appease the doge and the crusaders, garrisoned on the Lido, found themselves in a desperate situation. Venice would not let them return home unless they settled up, nor would it assist with the expedition to Egypt, even though (Venice had kept its part of the bargain) a fleet of ships had been built and was ready to set sail. We may assume that the summer of 1202, during which the soldiers were stranded on the Lido in the blazing heat of July and August, money and provisions ebbing away, was close to unendurable. The historian William Roscoe Thayer recreates it vividly: 'The Crusaders' camp on the Lido became a den of gamesters, harlots, and mountebanks, where the soldiery squandered their health and morals; disease took off many, and many deserted.'[9]

But just when things looked irretrievably dark for the crusaders, the doge made a shrewd proposal, described here by the eyewitness Robert of Clari, which was greeted with celebration on the Lido:

9   History repeated itself, admittedly without *filles de joie* or impromptu casinos, in the 19th century. On 19th July 1855 *The Times* published a letter from a correspondent who signed himself simply 'il Vecchio'. He described the plight of 20,000 Austrian soldiers stranded on the Lido. 'When they arrived they found they had not one tent, and most certainly no barracks. Exposed therefore, all day, to this clear cloudless burning sun—for the authorities in their wisdom had cut down all the trees—at night these poor devils were eaten up with mosquitoes [and when they woke up] they still retained the saturated clothes, and harboured millions of insects.' Bearing this in mind, it is probably safe to say that conditions on the Lido were as bad as that, if not considerably worse, in 1202.

The doge and his entourage paid a formal visit to the pilgrims at their camp on the Lido. When all had gathered together, he addressed them as follows. 'Men-at-arms,' he began, 'My people and I have taken counsel and come to a decision. You owe us thirty-six thousand marks…yet if you faithfully promise to pay this out of any booty you win on your expedition, we will give you leave to set sail forthwith.' When the soldiers of the Cross heard this, they were overcome with joy and prostrated themselves at the doge's feet, promising to agree to his terms. There was great rejoicing on the Lido that night and even the poorest soldiers lit their lamps in celebration. Many fastened great torches or arrangements of candles to their lances, fixing them in the ground near their tents, so that soon it seemed as though the entire encampment was ablaze.   (Tr. RS)

Doge Enrico, though well into his nineties and almost completely blind, made a great play of taking the Cross in San Marco, promising that he would come in person and serve in the front line, despite his age.

What most of the ordinary soldiers could not know, as they celebrated on the Lido, was the ulterior motive underlying the apparent magnanimity of Venice and the theatrical courage of its doge. The deal Dandolo had struck with their leaders depended on rather more than a share of the spoils. In exchange for Venice holding over the debt, the crusaders were to make a detour to Zara, a former Venetian colony in Dalmatia (modern Zadar, Croatia), and help the Venetians recapture it. This they did, but after the successful siege, a further plan was agreed on by the doge and the Frankish commanders, again designed to further Venice's interests rather than to advance the Crusade. This plan, to install Alexius Angelus, the exiled son of the deposed Byzantine emperor Isaac II, on the throne of Byzantium, was ambitious and grandiose, so much so that it completely eclipsed any idea of heading for Egypt. Instead, the crusaders set off for Constantinople, hoisted Alexius onto the throne—and when the new emperor found his coffers empty and could not pay them, they subjected the city to one of the bloodiest and most ferocious attacks in the history of the Crusades. The butchery inflicted by Christians on their fellow Christians matched and probably exceeded anything previously meted out to the Muslims. In his *Decline and Fall*, quoting the Byzantine chronicler Nicetas Choniates, Edward Gibbon describes the scene in Haghia Sophia:

After stripping the gems and pearls, they converted the chalices into drinking cups; their tables, on which they gamed and feasted, were covered with the pictures of Christ and the saints; and they trampled under foot the most venerable objects of the Christian worship. In the cathedral of St Sophia the ample veil of the sanctuary was rent asunder for the sake of the golden fringe; and the altar, a monument of art and riches, was broken in pieces and shared among the captors. Their mules and horses were laden with the wrought silver and gilt carvings which they tore down from the doors and pulpit; and if the beasts stumbled under the burden, they were stabbed by their impatient drivers, and the holy pavement streamed with their impure blood. A prostitute was seated on the throne of the patriarch; and the daughter of Belial, as she is styled, sang and danced in the church to ridicule the hymns and processions of the Orientals.

The sack of Constantinople enriched Venice, but the atrocities that accompanied it resonated throughout the Christian world for centuries. In 2001, Pope John Paul II wrote to Christodoulos, Archbishop of Athens, saying, 'It is tragic that the assailants, who set out to secure free access for Christians to the Holy Land, turned against their brothers in the faith. The fact that they were Latin Christians fills Catholics with deep regret.'

The martial and ceremonial function of the Lido became increasingly sophisticated over time. There were few buildings or residents to obstruct ceremonial, making the Lido an ideal and versatile backdrop for all kinds of celebrations. The most lavish of these was a reception for the French emperor Henri III in 1574. There had been previous reception parties on the

Lido for visiting dignitaries, but none as ambitious as this. A huge triumphal arch and loggia were designed by Palladio and decorated by Veronese and Tintoretto. Contemporary accounts of the preparations convey a palpable sense of time running out, corners being cut, the three great names of the Venetian Renaissance being pressed, willingly enough, into service as set designers. Palladio's triumphal arch and accompanying loggia were made of wood, painted to resemble marble. The paintings, by Veronese, Tintoretto and their assistants, comprised a sophisticated cycle celebrating Henri's military achievements and his stature as a Christian prince. After prayers at San Nicolò, Henri was ushered to the quay from where the state barge, the *Bucintoro*, would take him to San Marco. At that point, in a theatrical flourish, an attendant choir and orchestra struck up a sung eulogy. As the music began, all the churches of Venice rang their bells simultaneously, beckoning Henri and his entourage to San Marco. The festivities continued for several days and among the high points was a firework display, accompanied by music, emulating the eruption of Mt Etna.

Over a hundred years later, in 1685, similarly elaborate pageants were staged on the Lido by the Duke of Brunswick, who was determined to avoid the *longueurs* of confinement to a garrison. He organised 'music and dances in a little theatre, representing a forest glade, expressly erected for the occasion. The troops left for the scene of action, but the Duke preferred to linger on in the lazy atmosphere of the lagoon, amused by fêtes, serenades, and regattas.' He commissioned 'enormous mythological and symbolical figures decorated with a sumptuousness which was almost grotesque. At the winning post near the Palazzo Foscari a huge whale opened his jaws, whence issued a man dressed as a marine monster, who delivered the prizes.'[10]

Shortly after his conquest of Venice in 1797[11], Napoleon rode from one end of the Lido to the other, briskly making notes and giving instructions to his staff that the island should be shorn of any memory of Venetian supremacy and branded irrevocably with the insignia of France. He destroyed the *Bucintoro*, hunted down any pockets of resistance holding out in the lagoon, manned the Venetian fortifications with vigilant troops. Josephine paid a visit and for the first time in its his-

10   From *Venice*, Part III, Vol. I, by Pompeo Molmenti, translated from the Italian by Horatio F. Brown, British archivist and author of *In and Around Venice*.
11   It was from the Forte di Sant'Andrea, in April 1797, that the Venetians fired on the French warship *Libérateur d'Italie*, killing its commander Jean-Baptiste Laugier and giving Napoleon the *casus belli* he required to march on Venice. This episode marked the end of the Republic and is understandably much romanticised as the last instance of a shot being fired in anger by the servants of the doge. Napoleon would certainly have succeeded in finding a reason to subdue Venice if this episode had not presented one, but the story provides a fittingly theatrical end to a thousand years of fiercely upheld independence and uniquely crafted democratic government. In a complex series of treaties, Venice was first ceded to Austria by Napoleon. Subsequently it became, for a brief period, part of Napoleon's new Kingdom of Italy. Finally, after his defeat in 1815, it once again fell under Austrian rule.

tory the Lido was the scene of a celebration arranged under foreign rule. 'Madame Bonaparte,' relates Marshal Auguste de Marmont[12], 'was four days in Venice. I accompanied her hither. Three days were devoted to the most splendid feasts. On the first day there was a regatta, a species of amusement which seems reserved only to Venice, the queen of the sea…The second day we had a sea-excursion; a banquet had been prepared on the Lido: the population followed in barges adorned with wreaths and flowers, and to the sound of music re-echoing far and near.' Josephine prepared for the occasion in style, spending the equivalent of three months' military campaign wages for an entire army on clothes, jewellery and ladies-in-waiting. The high days of the Lido as an exclusive pleasure resort were not far away.

12   From Marmont's memoirs, appearing in *The Empress Josephine* (1867), a historical novel by Luise Mühlbach, the pen name of Clara Mundt (1814–73), translated into English by the Rev W. Binet.

A SPANKING GALLOP

What now? the Lido shall it be?
That none may say we didn't see
The ground which Byron used to ride on,
And do I don't know what beside on.
Ho, *barca*! here! and this light gale
Will let us run it with a sail.
Dipsychus, Arthur Hugh Clough

After Napoleon's defeat in 1815, life in Venice continued peacefully enough under Austrian rule and rich
foreigners again began to visit as they had done in the
days of the Grand Tour. The first notable British tourist to arrive in Venice after the Napoleonic Wars was
Lord Byron, who arrived in 1818 and set up a rackety
household in the Palazzo Mocenigo. There he abandoned himself to a vigorous round of creativity and dis-
solution. Each night, at his insistence, all the windows
of the Mocenigo were ablaze with candles. The clatter
of party revelry echoed across the Grand Canal, sometimes accompanied by the strident tirades of Byron's
earthy mistress, Margarita Cogni who, if not berating
the servants at the top of her voice, would usually be
nagging Byron on the boundless topic of his other mistresses. 'Very dark, tall,' (as Lord Byron says in a letter

to Murray) 'the Venetian face, very fine black eyes....
she was two and twenty years old...In the autumn, one
day, going to the Lido...we were overtaken by a heavy
squall...On our return, I found her on the open steps
of the Mocenigo palace, on the Grand Canal, with her
great black eyes flashing through her tears, and the long
dark hair, which was streaming drenched with rain
over her brows and breast. She was perfectly exposed
to the storm; and the wind blowing her hair and dress
about her thin figure, and the lightning flashing round
her, with the waves rolling at her feet, made her look
like Medea alighted from her chariot, or the Sibyl of
the tempest that was rolling around her, the only living
thing within hail at that moment except ourselves. On
seeing me safe, she did not wait to greet me, as might be
expected, but called out to me "Ah! can' della Madonna,
xe esto il tempo per andar' al' Lido?" (Ah! Dog of the
Virgin, is this a time to go to the Lido?)...'

The ground floor of the Mocenigo housed Byron's
menagerie. The stygian realm echoed with the growls
of Mutz, his much-loved mastiff, and the barks, howls,
shrieks and chattering of a growing collection of dogs,
birds and monkeys. They capered, snarled and twit-
tered in the gloom, their rattling cages arranged alongside Byron's rusting carriages with their once splendid
but now peeling armorials. It was small wonder that the
inner misanthrope in Byron—he was never a gregari-
ous character—craved solitude. The quiet shore of the

Lido seemed to offer a perfect retreat from the rigours of Venice. He therefore rented a disused fortification near Alberoni and transformed it into a makeshift stable.

> Talking of horses, by the way, I have transported my own, four in number, to the Lido (beach in English), a strip of some ten miles along the Adriatic, a mile or two from the city; so that I not only get a row in my gondola, but a spanking gallop of some miles daily along a firm and solitary beach, from the fortress to Malamocco, the which contributes considerably to my health and spirits. *Lord Byron to Moore (Letter 307)*

He spent agreeable mornings riding out alone or in the company of John Cam Hobhouse or the English consul, Belgrave Hoppner. Hobhouse records occasional meetings with other visitors on the otherwise desolate beach. A German banker and his companion tell them of Princess Charlotte's death which Byron finds unsettling and talks about for the rest of the day. They are accosted by a Contessa Tiretta, the Venetian courtesan who had for a while entangled herself with Byron's naïve and love-struck valet, Fletcher. When the Contessa, described by Hobhouse as a '*terra firma* countess', i.e. a whore, threatened suicide or, worse, a visit to England, Byron sent her packing with characteristic contempt.

He spent time on the Lido with Shelley, too, who commemorated their walks, rides and conversations in *Julian and Maddalo*, which evokes something of the solitariness and enchantment of the Lido in those days:

> I rode one evening with Count Maddalo
> Upon the bank of land which breaks the flow
> Of Adria towards Venice. A bare strand
> Of hillocks, heaped from ever-shifting sand,
> Matted with thistles and amphibious weeds,
> Such as from earth's embrace the salt ooze breeds,
> Is this; an uninhabited sea-side,
> Which the lone fisher, when his nets are dried,
> Abandons; and no other object breaks
> The waste but one dwarf tree and some few stakes
> Broken and unrepaired, and the tide makes
> A narrow space of level sand thereon,
> Where 'twas our wont to ride while day went down.
> This ride was my delight. I love all waste
> And solitary places; where we taste
> The pleasure of believing what we see
> Is boundless, as we wish our souls to be;
> And such was this wide ocean, and this shore
> More barren than its billows; and yet more
> Than all, with a remembered friend I love
> To ride as then I rode;—for the winds drove
> The living spray along the sunny air
> Into our faces; the blue heavens were bare,
> Stripped to their depths by the awakening north;
> And from the waves sound like delight broke forth

Harmonizing with solitude, and sent
Into our hearts aërial merriment.

'My rides would have been nothing without the Venetian sunsets,' Byron wrote to Thomas Medwin. 'Ask Shelley.' In the summer of 1818, when Shelley called on Byron in Venice, the first thing Byron did was to take him to the Lido. They talked for hours, mainly (Shelley reports) about Byron's affairs and literary work but also about their first meeting, two years previously, in Geneva. On the way back they stopped to look at the sun setting over Venice[13]. In Shelley's words,

> Half the sky
> Was roofed with clouds of rich emblazonry
> Dark purple at the zenith, which still grew
> Down the steep West into a wondrous hue
> Brighter than burning gold, even to the rent
> Where the swift sun yet paused in his descent
> Among the many-folded hills.

13   Lido sunsets have captivated others too. A.E. Housman, in *A Shropshire Lad*, described the 'green and sanguine shoals' off the Lido, an effect he also mentioned in a letter to his mother: 'the water declares its depth or shallowness by its colour: as the sun goes down it turns partly a golden green and partly a pale vermilion.' Wagner wrote to Mathilde von Wesendonck of his early evening gondola rides: 'The waning moon now rises late: at its full it furnished me fine comfort through agreeable sensations which I needed. After sunset I regularly took a gondola to meet it, toward the Lido, for the battle twixt day and night was always an entrancing vision in this limpid sky: to the right, amid the dusk-rose aether, gleamed kindly bright the evening star; the moon in full splendour cast its flashing net towards me in the sea.'

George Meredith, writing in 1861 to his friend Captain Maxse, describes a literary pilgrimage on which he retraced the steps of Byron and Shelley:

> My dear Maxse,—Behold a pretty picture, which is to tell you I have been in Venice, which you know so well, which is a dream and a seduction to the soul of me. I wish you had been there with me.—Now, mark the Campanile above, for you are to have it reproduced one day in illustrious verse. There did I conceive an Ode.—I have followed Byron's and Shelley's footsteps there (in Venice) on the Lido. Do you remember in *Julian and Maddalo*, where the two, looking towards the Euganean hills, see the great bell of the Insane Asylum swing in the sunset?[14] I found the exact spot. I have seldom felt melancholy so strongly as when standing there. You know I despise melan-

14   'Look, Julian, on the west, and listen well
If you hear not a deep and heavy bell.'
I looked, and saw between us and the sun
A building on an island,—such a one
As age to age might add, for uses vile,
A windowless, deformed and dreary pile;
And on the top an open tower, where hung
A bell, which in the radiance swayed and swung;
We could just hear its hoarse and iron tongue;
The broad sun sunk behind it, and it tolled
In strong and black relief. 'What we behold
Shall be the madhouse and its belfry tower,'
Said Maddalo; 'and ever at this hour
Those who may cross the water hear that bell,
Which calls the maniacs each one from his cell.'

choly, but the feeling came. I love both those poets; and with my heart given to them I felt as if I stood in a dead and useless time. So are we played with sometimes! At that hour your heart was bursting with a new passion, and the past was as smoke flitting away from a fired-off old contemptible gun.

Byron resented any unexpected intrusion into his Lido idyll. He was, one might say, one of the first victims of the modern cult of celebrity, besieged wherever he went by an adoring public, mostly young women. When it became common knowledge that he rode out on the Lido nearly every day, gondolas of eager tourists made their way over—a serious undertaking in those days, when the trip might easily have taken over two hours—in the hope of seeing their hero.

The fact is, that I hold in utter abhorrence any contact with the travelling English, as my friend the Consul General Hoppner, and the Countess Benzoni (in whose house the *Conversazione* mostly frequented by them is held), could amply testify, were it worthwhile. I was persecuted by these tourists even to my riding ground at Lido, and reduced to the most disagreeable circuits to avoid them. At Madame Benzoni's I repeatedly refused to be introduced to them;—of a thousand such presentations pressed upon me, I accepted two, and both were to Irish women.

A visitor he may have found less tiresome, though he never met him, was the German philosopher Arthur Schopenhauer: 'Goethe had given me a letter of introduction for Byron. I was to deliver it to him, in Venice. As I went for a walk on the Lido with my beloved lady, she exclaimed, with depths of emotion: "Ecco! il poeta inglese!" (Look! The English Poet!). At this instant, Byron was riding towards us, and my lady could not, all day, forget his appearance. I decided then not to hand over this letter from Goethe to Byron, so much I was afraid of being cuckold. I regret it.'

Byron spent a further two years in Venice, enduring the sightseers and providing his followers with an unforgettable flourish. On a fine morning in June 1818, he and two other swimmers raced from the Lido to Venice. His companions dropped out long before the agreed finishing point, but Byron pressed on and won the race. He recalled this feat in a letter to John Murray: 'I had been in the water by my watch without help or rest and never touching ground or boat for four hours and twenty minutes.' In an earlier letter, to his banker and literary agent Douglas Kinnaird, he boasted that:

I have lately had a long swim (beating an Italian all to bubbles) of more than four miles, from Lido to the other end of the Grand Canal, that is the part which enters from Mestri [sic]. I won by a good three quarters of a mile, and as many quarters of an hour, knocking the Chevalier up and coming in myself quite fresh; the fellow had swum the Beresina in the Bonaparte Campaign, and thought of coping with 'us Youth'[15], but it would not do.

Every year seasoned swimmers attempt Byron's feat with the full blessing of the authorities, but from time to time a maverick surfaces who tries to emulate him single-handed and without permission. The most distinguished of these was the late Hans Brill, librarian of the Royal Academy of Arts, who attempted Byron's route at the age of 72. Sadly, though he was very fit and might well have completed the course, he was fished out of the lagoon by a detachment of over-solicitous *carabinieri*.

Writing to Belgrave Hoppner from Bologna in 1819, Byron expressed a wish, never to be fulfilled, that he be buried on the Lido.

I found, too, such a pretty epitaph in the Certosa cemetery, or rather two: one was

> *Martini Luigi*
> *Implora pace'*

the other,

> *Lucrezia Picini*
> *Implora eterna quiete.'*

15   Byron is quoting Falstaff, *Henry IV Part I*, II ii 85.

That was all; but it appears to me that these two and three words comprise and compress all that can be said on the subject,—and then, in Italian, they are absolute music. They contain doubt, hope, and humility; nothing can be more pathetic than the '*implora*' and the modesty of the request;—they have had enough of life—they want nothing but rest—they implore it, and '*eterna quiete*'. It is like a Greek inscription in some good old heathen 'City of the Dead'. Pray, if I am shovelled into the Lido churchyard in your time, let me have the '*implora pace*,' and nothing else, for my epitaph. I never met with any, ancient or modern, that pleased me a tenth part so much.

THE COCKNEY VILLAGE

By the end of the 18th century the Lido had become popular as a resort for family bathing and picnicking, so much so that in July 1794 the *Gazzetta Urbana Veneta* issued the following bulletin: 'We warn that the Lido is not only dangerous due to the possibility of stray cattle that have escaped, but also for certain thieves that pretend to amuse themselves on the beach and instead steal the silver buckles from the swimmers' shoes or the money from the pockets of their clothes left in piles on the beach. Keep your eyes open. Be careful.' After the Napoleonic Wars, under the Austrian regime, the beaches became the scene of a new phenomenon, known in dialect as the *Luni di Lio*, 'Lido Mondays'. Every Monday Venetians would flock to the beach to bathe, walk, flirt or exercise. But it was not until the 1850s that bathing was seriously commercialised. When that happened, the development of public bathing establishments, the *stabilimenti*, triggered an outpouring of indignation from cultured visitors who had come to regard the Lido as their own sacrosanct paradise, a strip of wild, elemental shore that should remain forever exclusive and untouched. The most vehement and informative complaints came from three very different but equally insistent sources, John Ruskin, Henry James

and the then very popular English novelist Louise de la
Ramée, better known by her pen name, Ouida.

All three deplored what they saw as the seedy vulgarity of the *stabilimenti* and the raucous intrusion of
the steam launches. These, though they dramatically
cut travelling time to the Lido, were intrusively noisy
and dirty. For hundreds of years the trip from Rialto
had taken two or three hours, depending on whether
one went by oar or sail. Now, large groups of trippers
could be ferried across within half an hour at regular
intervals. Today, the chugging of *vaporetti* is thought of
affectionately as being as much a part of the Venetian
soundscape as church bells and the lapping of water
against the steps of a shadowy *sottoportego*. Then, it
was a different matter. Belching smoke, bells, whistles,
the grunt of engines, the clank of chains and the bel-
lowing of the pilots, all these were widely considered
to be the devil's work and to mark the beginning of
the end. Ruskin, ever paternalistic, saw the reworked
Lido as a new hell where the intrinsically noble working man would be brutalised by the gimcrack lure of
cheap tourism. Henry James deplored the obliteration
of the desolate sands by the 'cockney village' of bathing huts and cheap restaurants. Ouida agreed with both
of them, and in addition highlighted what she saw as
the potentially contaminating impact of progress on the
delicate microeconomy of the lagoon: in the wake of
steam, what would become of the gondoliers? For some

gondoliers, as will be seen, this was a question soon to
be answered, particularly in the case of those who were
fortunate enough to strike up acquaintance with foreign
residents or tourists.

John Ruskin married Euphemia Gray, 'Effie', in 1848
and they spent the first leg of their honeymoon in Venice.
The distressing and embarrassing breakdown of their
marriage is well documented. If one admires, as many
do, both of these appealing yet ill-matched characters,
then Effie's upbeat and optimistic account of the trip to
Venice makes sad reading in the light of differences to
come. She for her part tries to fit in with John's rigor-
ous and anti-social work schedule: in Effie's account we
glimpse him in their box at the Fenice, scribbling at his
notes while everyone else is watching the ballet. John
for his part joins Effie on excursions to the Lido where
they enjoy picnics together, walks and the company of
friends. But even at this early stage they were leading
separate lives. While Effie set about enjoying the round
of balls, concerts and entertainments laid on by Austro-
Hungarian high society, John continued his meticulous
record of the city in words and pictures, eventually to
be published as his masterpiece, *The Stones of Venice*.

Effie's descriptions of outings to the Lido, to be found
in her letters to friends and family, are enchanting. 'We
all went to Lido on Saturday. It was a most exquisite
day and the Adriatic lay stretched out in one unbroken
sheet of blue. John and the Austrian [a friend] walked

one way along the shore discussing the formation of sand banks and the theories of the tides, and Charlotte & I went in the opposite direction for about two hours and lastly lay down among the long grass and gathered shells until our Handkerchiefs were quite full.' After a while, the men rejoined them and they spent an agreeable afternoon catching miniature crabs, 'racing' them on the beach. On the way back, they 'passed a great Austrian man of war covered at the top with Sailors clustered like bees about the rigging and singing to their hearts content.' Yet, despite the idyllic tone, there are shadows of decay: 'One day I went with John over to Lido and found such lovely violets amongst the ancient Jews' burying ground. John said they smelt of *old clothes* but I found them as sweet as growing in Christian Lanes...'

During their stay, the Ruskins met and became lifelong friends with the English scholar and antiquarian Rawdon Lubbock Brown, who had edited the despatches of Sebastiano Giustiniani, the Venetian ambassador to the court of Henry VIII. John and Effie helped him publish this work and establish himself as an expert on Venetian history[16]. No dry antiquary, Brown encour-

16   As a result, he was commissioned by Lord Palmerston to calendar all of the Venetian state papers that had some bearing on English affairs. This vast project enabled him to stay in Venice for the rest of his life. Brown was a keen sailor and oarsman and kept a *sandalo*, a small, flat-bottomed Venetian boat, in which he could often be seen, his immediately recognisable form silhouetted against the skyline, as described in a letter to *The Times* from a correspondent signing him or herself simply 'E.E.', 8th September 1883:

aged Effie's love of swimming and it is thanks to him that she was the first of the season's bathers on the Lido in 1850: 'I find the heat so strengthening and I have not been so well for long as these few last very hot days. I believe bathing at the Lido has a good deal to do with it. Nobody has begun, yet I thought it was quite warm enough and that it would be a pity to leave Venice without having a few dips in the Adriatic. Mr Brown kindly lent me two old sails with which my Gondoliers construct in a few minutes a very serviceable sort of tent where, with Mary's [the maid's] aid, I undress & dress. The sea is delightfully warm and the bottom such beautiful smooth sand that I enjoy my bathe excessively.'

Ruskin, meanwhile, pressed on with his architectural survey of Venice, in which he was high-handed in his views of the architecture on the Lido. Nothing less than full-blown Gothic of the highest calibre would satisfy him and he predictably dismissed San Nicolò al Lido as being 'of no interest' (the 'of no interest' tag appears again and again in *The Stones of Venice* and it is too easy, sometimes, to fall in with Ruskin's passionately outlined prejudices). His responses to natural beauty are effective, though framed in poetic convention, as when he

'equally, day after day and year after year, did his tall, slim and well-knit figure, after his task was done, appear on the Grand Canal, rowing himself, gondolier fashion, to the Lido.' His scholarship was intense, delivering revelations that are small but unignorable. A good example is his disclosure that the three mulberries in the Moro arms equate to the three strawberries on Desdemona's handkerchief.

memorably describes the effect of the animated façade of the Doge's Palace, on which:

> …as if in ecstasy, the crests of the arches break into a marble foam, and toss themselves far into the blue sky in flashes and wreaths of sculptured spray, as if the breakers on the Lido shore had been frost-bound before they fell and the sea nymphs had inlaid them with coral and amethyst.

Ruskin's pronouncements on what he saw as the new barbarism are set out in *Fors Clavigera*, a collection of high-minded and prescriptive letters addressed to the British working man. In Letter 19, dated June 1872, he is unable to concentrate because of the whistling of the steam boat taking passengers to the Lido, a complaint that brings to mind his remark that Dickens was 'a pure modernist', 'a leader of the steam-whistle party *par excellence*'. In Letter 43, he complains of the brutalisation of the Venetian worker, offering an argument that is remorselessly nostalgic, founded on a romantic view of Venetian history. It is sad, he muses, that a man whose ancestors fought with Dandolo at the gates of Constantinople should be reduced to taking a day trip to the Lido, where his spirit would be dampened by listening to brass band medleys from Gounod's *Faust*.

It is too easy to dismiss Ruskin on the strength of these outpourings and there is, perhaps, something to be said for adopting the tolerant approach recommended by Henry James: 'There is no better reading at Venice… than Ruskin, for every true Venice-lover can separate the wheat from the chaff. The narrow theological spirit, the moralism *à tout propos*, the queer provincialities and pruderies, are mere wild weeds in a mountain of flowers.' It may be that one of the brightest and freshest flowers on that mountain, a souvenir of Ruskin at his best, is the following description of his mischievous dog, Wisie, and his escapades on the Lido:

He was a white spitz, exactly like Carpaccio's dog in the picture of St Jerome; and he came to me from a young Austrian officer, who had got tired of him, the Count Thun, who fell afterward at Solferino. Before the dog was used enough to us, George and I took him to Lido to give him a little sea bath. George was holding him by his forepaws upright among the little crisp breakers. Wisie snatched them out of his hands, and ran at full speed into Fairyland, like Frederick the Great at Mollwitz. He was lost on Lido for three days and nights, living by petty larceny, the fishermen and cottagers doing all they could to catch him, but they told me 'he ran like a hare and leaped like a horse.' At last, either overcome by hunger or having made up his mind that even my service was preferable to liberty on Lido, he took the deep water in broad day-light, and swam straight for Venice. A fisherman saw him from a distance, rowed after him, took him, tired among the weeds, and brought him to me, the Madonna della Salute having been propitious to his repentant striving with the sea. From that time he became an obedient and affectionate dog, though of extremely self-willed and self-possessed character. I was then living on the north side of St Mark's Place, and he used to sit outside the window on the ledge at the base of its pillars the greater part of the day, observant of the manners and customs of Venice.

For Henry James, as his biographer Leon Edel puts it, 'Venice was one of the greatest topographical love affairs'. A regular visitor, he observed with dismay the quickening encroachment of tourism. His views on what he saw as the atrocities inflicted on Venice in the name of progress are well-documented in *Italian Hours*, a collection of travel writing published in 1909. These essays span four decades and provide an intriguing and infectious view of James's love affair with Italy and Italians. Though he revised the collection from time to time in an attempt to give it shape and unity, part of its charm lies in the unstudied changes of style and emphasis over the years, as James celebrates a fresh enthusiasm or seizes on a new *bête noire*:

May in Venice is better than April, but June is best of all. Then the days are hot, but not too hot, and

the nights are more beautiful than the days. Then
Venice is rosier than ever in the morning and more
golden than ever as the day descends. She seems to
expand and evaporate, to multiply all her reflections
and iridescences. Then the life of her people and the
strangeness of her constitution become a perpetual
comedy, or at least a perpetual drama. Then the gondola is your sole habitation, and you spend days between sea and sky. You go to the Lido, though the
Lido has been spoiled. When I first saw it, in 1869, it
was a very natural place, and there was but a rough
lane across the little island from the landing-place to
the beach. There was a bathing-place in those days,
and a restaurant, which was very bad, but where in
the warm evenings your dinner didn't much matter
as you sat letting it cool on the wooden terrace that
stretched out into the sea. To-day the Lido is a part
of united Italy and has been made the victim of vil-
lainous improvements. A little cockney village has
sprung up on its rural bosom and a third-rate boule-
vard leads from Santa Elisabetta to the Adriatic. There
are bitumen walks and gas-lamps, lodging-houses,
shops and a *teatro diurno*. The bathing-establishment
is bigger than before, and the restaurant as well; but
it is a compensation perhaps that the cuisine is no
better. Such as it is, however, you won't scorn occasionally to partake of it on the breezy platform under
which bathers dart and splash, and which looks out

to where the fishing-boats, with sails of orange and crimson, wander along the darkening horizon. The beach at the Lido is still lonely and beautiful, and you can easily walk away from the cockney village. The return to Venice in the sunset is classical and indispensable, and those who at that glowing hour have floated toward the towers that rise out of the lagoon will not easily part with the impression.

An altogether more volatile character than James was Louise de la Ramée, known as Ouida, who, despite her exotic name and pen name, was born in Bury St Edmunds, Suffolk, England. A restless spirit, she was quick to abandon the unstimulating backwaters of Bury where, she claimed, 'the inhabitants are driven to ringing their own doorbells lest they rust from lack of use.' She settled in Italy in 1874 and remained there until her death in 1908, producing a respectable oeuvre of over 40 books including novels, critical essays and children's stories. She was an untiring supporter of Italian Independence—the newly unified Italy was still finding its feet when Ouida arrived there—and a committed lover of Venice. She was also a prolific and accomplished writer of articles for and letters to *The Times*:

A very little care and good taste would make the Lido a paradise; it has a fine beach of fine sand, meadows of the freshest, greenest grass, and superb trees, yet so ill or ignorantly is it dealt with that the military occupation of the Santa Elisabetta side of it, and the casino and tramway of the Santa Maria side, ruin its beauty and deprive it of its charm. The lonely sand, with the wild Adriatic rollers breaking upon them, and the acacia-thickets and woods which Byron loved are there, almost unexampled in their union of the marine and sylvan landscape; but they are alone and unaided in their struggle against the vulgarity and destruction which seem the inevitable accompaniments to modern life. Nature has done so much for the Lido that man has only to respect her work to let it be a perfect haven of rest and loveliness, but alas! One side of it is given over to the soldiers and the other to the brass bands, the sandwich papers, and the bathing machines.   (*22nd September 1885.*)

Ouida was capable of carefully judged lyricism too, describing the distinctive fishing boats of the lagoon which were then a familiar sight around the Lido:

On the horizon there would be a long, tall line of fishing boats, their red sails flashing against the pearl grey of the sky like the painted wings of great moths, spread for flight; as you gazed at them, they seemed to stand there motionless; then, as you looked away for a moment and looked back again, one of them would have vanished suddenly, as if it had gone down

into the sea. And the water, which rippled so gently against the sand at my feet, had something of the
gentleness of colour of that water which meanders
about the shores of Ireland. It shone, and seemed to
grow whiter and whiter, as it stretched out towards
the horizon, where the fishing-boats stood up in their
long, tall line against the sky; it had the delicacy, the
quietude of the lagoon, with, in those bright sails, the
beckoning of a possible escape from the monotony of
too exquisite things.

Despite the reactionary and nostalgic opinions of
Ruskin, James and Ouida, there were eloquent advo-
cates of the new resort. Among these was the English
governess Nellie Ryan, a companion in the household
of Archduke Karl Stephan, a cousin of Franz Joseph and
Admiral of the Austrian fleet. Her engaging memoir, *My
Years at the Austrian Court* (1915), recalls the family's
days on the Lido. There is little evidence of the 'cockney
village' despised by James in the plutocratic scenes she
vividly recreates:

We all knew His Imperial Highness's horror of fashionable resorts and smart crowds. After so much
sightseeing, Archduchess Maria Theresa then proposed three weeks' calm and quiet in Venice, and
bathing in the famous Lido. That was a great joy to
all. Summer in Venice was ideal, especially in the ear-

ly mornings, and late at night. Practically the whole morning was spent out on the Lido, where we were taken each time by a little steam-launch. Once again we seemed back in the land of gaiety and fashion, for we soon found the Lido was one of those famous bathing-places where the wearing of smart costumes, head-gear, and foot-gear, is far more important than being able to swim well. But, as the Archduke argued, we should not stay on the Lido merely go there each day for the bathing. There was a great terrace built out over that part of the sea where the bathing took place, and beautiful little bathing-houses were arranged along under another wide projection. On the terrace a fine military band played morning and afternoon; gay luncheons and teas were served, and all the smart world from many European countries was to be seen daily, each trying to outdo the other in wondrous and gorgeous creations. All the Imperial Family revelled in the bathing; the water was so warm and delicious, that an hour or more was always spent idling in the gentle waves of the beautiful Lido.

It is a mistake to suppose that beach life in the 19th century was an uninterrupted idyll. There were ludicrous and undignified episodes too, featuring distinguished tourists whose behaviour in the 1880s prefigured the devil-may-care pranking and capering of the smart set in the 1920s. Richard Burton, the Arabist, explorer and pornographer, appeared on the beach in 1887, bursting with energy, larking about with V. Lovett Cameron, the Africa explorer. They built sandcastles. 'Look, nurse,' bawled Burton to his wife, 'see what Cammy and I have done!' 'If you please, nursey,' whined Cameron, 'Dick's snatched away my spade.'[17] At that moment Lord Aberdare, President of the Royal Geographical Society, passed by accompanied by a party of grave antiquaries and geographers.

Others, particularly Englishmen, remained comically immune to the charms of the Lido, seeing in every grain of sand, blade of grass or glimmer of moonlight a reassuring reminder of life at home. Francis Palgrave, the compiler of the 'Golden Treasury' of verse, described the lagoon as having 'the complex character of the Sussex shores' and the Lido as having the 'appearance of meadows bordering the South-hampton River'. The English judge J.A. Strahan found himself transported back to his youth in the English Midlands by an unlikely episode at the Grand Hotel des Bains:

The favourite song sung on festive occasions on the Midland was *John Peel*, and I never hear it till this day but it 'stirs my heart like a trumpet'. The last time it reached my ears was one night on the Lido of Venice in the year before the war. I had been spending the

17   Quoted in *The Life of Sir Richard Burton* by Thomas Wright.

day in the city, and returned very late to the Hotel des
Bains. As I was leaving the next morning for Bologna,
on going to my bedroom I went out on my balcony to
have a farewell look at the Adriatic. Above me a great
Italian moon filled the still warm air with light, below me the sea shimmered like a lake of quicksilver,
and away on my left the white summits of the Julian
Alps stood up like spear-heads against the purple sky.
As I looked about me a pleasant English voice began
from a neighbouring balcony to sing that old hunting
song, and immediately I forgot the moonlight and the
Adriatic and the Alps, and was once more back at
my first grand night dinner on the Midland: we were
at Nottingham, that song was being sung, and the
whole mess was joining in the chorus.[18]

No less inward-looking is the Bulgarian revolutionary
Insarov in Turgenev's *On the Eve*. He exudes a Slavic
melancholy that the winter beauties of the Lido are inadequate to dispel, walking moodily along the beach
with Elena as the foaming breakers leave their characteristic debris of broken shells and seaweed on the
shore. Is it too cold for him, she wonders? No, perish
the thought! What sort of soldier would he be if he were
unable to endure the cold? He has come to the beach,
he says, to be nearer to his country. There it is over the

18   *The Bench and Bar of England: The Life of a Lawyer,* J.A. Strahan, 1919.

water, he tells her, pointing out towards the Adriatic. And the chill wind blows in from the East.

But despite the presence of a few real and fictional detractors the Lido had become, by the end of the 19th century, an internationally known resort, associated in the popular mind with carefree, somewhat raffish and increasingly fashionable holidays.

There were, inevitably, tragedies amid the holiday gaiety, and ghosts to accompany them. In 1883, three sisters committed suicide by walking into the sea at the Lido. It seems that after the death of their mother they were heartbroken, unable to carry on. The eldest was very pretty—strikingly beautiful, it was said—but suffered from failing eyesight and was prone to epileptic fits. Contemporary reports tell us that immediately before leaving home for the beach, the girls had been reading Manzoni's *I Promessi Sposi*—it had been left open at the page describing Lucia's sadness at leaving her native home. The *Colonist* newspaper (9th January 1884) was less than charitable: 'Venice is not a place to move any but a sentimental tourist to melancholy. The "ghost by the shores of the sea, so pale, so quiet" of Mr Ruskin's rhetoric is a very enjoyable town to live in. This makes the determined conduct of the three girls all the more inexplicable.' The ghosts of the sisters (their name was Angeli) are said to walk the sands at twilight.

A no less unsettling ghost awaits unwary young men walking along the Lungomare at night, that of the young woman who, in 1886, was struck dead by lightning in the arms of her lover, at a dance held in a private hotel. Her charred spectre has been seen on the Lido's shores and promenades, searching for a new partner and a final dance. Finally, beckoning the solitary walker from a distant age, we see on the beach the shade of Edward Courtenay, a Protestant exile from the court of Queen Mary, who met his death in mysterious circumstances in 1556:

Courtenay's death was compassed, not by steel at Venice, as was intended, but by poison at Padua, from which city Peter Vannes, the Queen's ambassador, wrote her an account of it on the 18th September 1556, commencing thus:—'The Earl of Devonshire died little more than an hour ago. In the middle of August whilst at Venice, where he was made much of, for his recreation he happened to go to Lido to see his hawk fly upon a waste. There he was suddenly overtaken by a great tempest of wind and rain, so that he could not return to Venice by his gondola, but was forced to take a searcher's boat which had arrived there by chance, and so got to Venice, being body and legs very thinly clothed, refusing to change them with any warmer garment.' About five days after, as he told Vannes, he had a fall on the stairs of his house, but, feeling well and suffering no pain, came hither. To avoid the tediousness of the water and save horses he took the worst way and came by 'a certain waggons called coches, very shaking and uneasy to my judgment,' arriving on a Saturday night. Hearing of his coming, went to visit him next day, and found him very weak. After that he grew daily worse and worse, avoiding friends' visitations as a speech molest to him, and drew himself to the counsel of two of the best physicians here, and entered into a continual great hot ague, some time more vehement than at another. He was always diligently attended. Has charged his servants in her Majesty's name to take a true inventory of the small moveables he had, and especially that all writings or letters that he had here or at Venice shall be put in assurance to await the royal commands.

From *'Preface', Calendar of State Papers Relating to English Affairs in the Archives of Venice, Vol. 6: 1555–58 (1877), pp. VII–LXIII.*

It is said that the spirit of the sad, handsome young earl paces the sands of the Lido to this day, longing for the time when the truth surrounding his mysterious death will finally be revealed.

A GENTLEMAN
SAUNTERING BY

I know nothing of Venice except that the wise are said to stay at the Lido, where there is ripping bathing and no mosquitoes, and go over to Venice when they want to. It is quite close, much closer than the Isle of Wight is to Portsmouth and much jollier. I hate the Isle of Wight.
Adolphus ('Dollie') Heathcote, in E.V. Lucas's
Over Bemerton's: An Easy-Going Chronicle

Adolphus had unwittingly grasped, if nothing else, how conveniently close the Lido is to Rialto, how easily the Guardi-sated sophisticate might flee the tyrannous grind of churches, palaces and galleries. Among the first and most *soigné* tourists to praise the beach as an antidote to high art was the English sculptor Lord Ronald Gower: 'When jaded with too much sight-seeing, one gets a longing for unadorned nature; then how easy to cross to the Lido, and to follow the tide for miles along those sands on which Byron loved to ride…' Gower, a refined, exuberant and uninhibited homosexual, was the model for Lord Henry Wotton in Oscar Wilde's *The Picture of Dorian Gray*. Upon visiting Venice he quickly joined the circle of two other English homosexuals, John Addington Symonds and Horatio Brown, who showed him the sights: 'With Horatio in his gondola to the Lido. We returned in a golden glow of sunset splendour, the sea the hue of amethyst and topaz—Santa Maria della Salute standing out dark against a brilliant golden sky. Horatio declared it one of the most perfect evenings he'd had ever seen here!'

The status of homosexuals in Venice had for centuries been troubled. In the early days of the Republic, sodomy was a grave crime, unrelentingly punished by the Council of Ten. The sinister magistrates who monitored public morality and dealt with transgressors were known as the *Signori di Notte*, the 'Lords of the Night', so called because the mischief they sought to punish was most likely to take place under cover of darkness—theft, murder, escape from the galleys, 'dancing by moonlight' (i.e. witchcraft) and sodomy. By the mid-15th century, sodomy was so prevalent in the Venetian navy that the Senate feared that the fleet might be destroyed in an act of divine retribution, an outcome that would have conclusively put paid to Venetian mercantile supremacy. Deterrents were called for and for a long time the punishment for sodomy was to be burnt alive, in some cases commuted to the following less theatrical but no less unpleasant fate. A prisoner would be gagged and bound, his legs weighted with ballast of Istrian marble, a sack placed over his head. The executioners would row him by night out to the chill, jet black waters of Canale degli Orfani off the Lido.

By the end of the 18th century these disciplines were little more than a distant curiosity. By then the Republic had reached a pitch of decadence so intense that prostitution was openly practised and it was often impossible to tell whether a prostitute was male or female. Sodomy—and many other forms of illegal sexual activity—became widely tolerated. As a result, Venice soon became popular with sexual tourists escaping from the constraints of their own countries. Furtive bourgeois pederasts from the chilly Protestant climes north of the Alps lurked around beaches and *sottoporteghi*, their faces safely concealed behind carnival masks. While the authorities turned a blind eye to the antics of these well-heeled visitors, ordinary transgressors were less fortunate. Soldiers and sailors, often eager to supplement their meagre pay through prostitution, were routinely incarcerated in the Lido's new Corpo della Disciplina: 'There is a military prison on the Lido at Venice,' reported John Addington Symonds, 'where incorrigible lovers of their own sex, amongst other culprits, are confined. A man here said: "All our loves in this place are breech-loaders."' But despite these setbacks, the Lido was becoming well known as a discreet and agreeable place on which to solicit or be solicited.

In the summer of 1889 the celebrated Prussian bodybuilder Eugen Sandow was bathing at the Lido. Sandow, the author of *Strength and How To Obtain It*, had been a hit in Italy, photographed striking heroic poses while twirling his Indian clubs. Bronzed, hyper-muscular, with an eighteen-inch neck, he stepped out of the sea and made his way to the shore. 'I had quitted the water' he reports, 'and was making my way up the beach when I noticed I had become the particular attraction for a gentleman sauntering by. As I apologised in passing him, he stopped to compliment me upon what he was pleased to term my "perfect physique and beauty of form".' The sauntering gentleman was the American artist E. Aubrey Hunt, a painter of Adriatic views. He took Sandow under his wing and introduced him to an elegant circle of friends, smoothing a few of the bodybuilder's rougher edges. According to a catty member of the circle, Hunt subsequently learned that Sandow could 'do much more with his muscles than a painter might suppose…', though there was no evidence of a physical relationship. Hunt memorably painted Sandow as a gladiator in ancient Rome. The somewhat bemused and nervously musclebound Prussian poses awkwardly, wearing nothing but a skimpy leopardskin loincloth.

The advent of the steamboats provoked an enormous outcry from many quarters. One of the most interesting issues, triggering many letters to *The Times* from Ouida and others, was the fate of the gondoliers. There was a very real danger, said Ouida, that they might be made redundant by the steamboats, especially since they had for centuries held an unchallengeable monopoly on the transportation of tourists to the Lido and the islands of the lagoon. In reality, the gondoliers proved resourceful. The more enterprising went as far afield as the Chicago Trade Fair where they were duly fêted. Others took their chances in the homosexual underworld of Venice where, if they were lucky, they might find a civilised and generous foreign patron of a literary and romantic disposition. The most celebrated gondolier to benefit from the new cult of *gondolismo* among affluent homosexual expatriates was Angelo Fusato, who became and remained for many years the faithful companion of John Addington Symonds. In his frank memoirs, written shortly before his death in 1893 but, at his insistence, published posthumously, Symonds relates how he met Angelo on the Lido:

> One afternoon I chanced to be sitting with my friend Horatio Brown in a little backyard to the wineshop of Fighetti at S. Elisabetta on the Lido. Gondoliers patronise this place, because Fighetti, a muscular giant, is a hero among them. He has won I do not know how many flags in their regattas. While we were drinking our wine Brown pointed out to me two men in white gondolier uniform, with the enormously broad black hat which was then fashionable. They were servants of a General de Horsey; and one of them was strikingly handsome. The following description of him, written a few days after our first meeting, represents with fidelity the impression he made on my imagination.

He was tall and sinewy, but very slender—for these Venetian gondoliers are rarely massive in their strength. Each part of the man is equally developed by the exercise of rowing; and their bodies are elastically supple, with free sway from the hips and a Mercurial poise upon the ankle. Angelo showed these qualities almost in exaggeration. Moreover, he was rarely in repose, but moved with a singular brusque grace.—Black broad-brimmed hat thrown back upon his matted *zazzera* of dark hair.—Great fiery grey eyes, gazing intensely, with compulsive effluence of electricity—the wild glance of a Triton.—Short blond moustache; dazzling teeth; skin bronzed, but showing white and delicate through open front and sleeves of lilac shirt.—The dashing sparkle of this splendour, who looked to me as though the sea waves and the sun had made him in some hour of secret and unquiet rapture, was somehow emphasised by a curious dint dividing his square chin—a cleft that harmonised with smile on lips and steady fire in eyes.—By the way, I do not know what effect it would have upon a reader to compare eyes to opals. Yet Angelo's eyes, as I met them, had the flame and vitreous intensity of opals, as though the quintessential colour of Venetian waters were vitalised in them and fed from inner founts of passion.—This marvellous being had a rough hoarse voice which, to develop the simile of a sea-god, might have screamed in storm or whispered raucous messages from crests of tossing waves. He fixed and fascinated me. In these waking dreams I was at one time a woman whom he loved, at another a companion in his trade—always somebody and something utterly different from myself; and as each distracting fancy faded in the void of fact and desert of reality, I writhed in the clutches of chimaera, thirsted before the tempting phantasmagoria of Maya. My good sense rebelled, and told me that I was morally a fool and legally a criminal. But the love of the impossible rises victorious after each fall given it by sober sense. Man must be a demigod of volition, a very Hercules, to crush the life out of that Antaeus, lifting it aloft from the soil of instinct and of appetite which eternally creates it new in his primeval nature.

Another literary visitor to Venice who regularly employed a favourite gondolier was A.E. Housman. He wrote regularly to his mother, Lucy, and in 1900 tells her of his gondolier Andrea's domestic problems:

My gondolier expressed a wish that he were your son. He wanted me to come to Venice next Christmas, and I explained that at Christmas I went to see you; and then he made this remark. The reason is, that if he were your son he would be well off and would have no family to provide for: so at least he says. At present he has to earn a living for one wife, two sisters, one mother, one mother-in-law, and half an uncle (who was once a champion oarsman and is now paralysed); which is pretty good for a young man of twenty-three who has had one eye kicked out by a horse.

Andrea has been the source of much speculation but there is no compelling evidence that he and Housman were lovers. Though Housman helped Andrea out with cash from time to time, this seems to have been a genuine act of compassion rather than the by-product of a full-blown love affair of the kind embarked on by Symonds and Brown. There was, for a while, an internet group whose members devoted themselves solely to the question of Andrea. One of the wilder misapprehensions aired was that Housman, a professor of Latin and Greek, had taken the gondolier back to Cambridge University and set him up in Trinity College. Had Andrea brought his gondola with him, someone wondered, and swanned to and fro on the Cam? Though he never gained Trinity Great Court, Andrea did earn himself a place in one of the verses published posthumously as *More Poems*. Housman refers to the Campanile of San Marco and to its dramatic collapse in July 1902, using the event to symbolise the eventual severance of his own relationship with Venice:

It looks to north and south,
    It looks to east and west;

It guides to Lido mouth
    The steersman of Triest.
Andrea, fare you well;
    Venice, farewell to thee.
The tower that stood and fell
    Is not rebuilt in me.

Writing to his sister Katherine in 1926, Housman says of Venice that '...everything there is better in reality than in memory. I first saw it on a romantic evening after sunset in 1900, and I left it on a sunshiny morning, and I shall not go there again.'

Not to be outdone by Symonds, Housman or anyone else, Horatio Brown dedicated a book, *Life on the Lagoons*, to his gondolier: 'To my Gondolier, Antonio Salin, my constant companion in Venice and Venetia'. Antonio and his family moved into the house near Rialto where Horatio Brown lived with his mother. This somewhat unusual domestic arrangement, with the gondolier firmly *in situ*, worked well for some years, though it robbed Brown of the evident pleasure of the clandestine visits he had paid Antonio in the past: 'I found the door, and at the top of the little staircase there was Antonio, his head fresh from a basin of water, all his masses of hair tossed back and dripping, like Bacchus stepped from Tintoret's loveliest picture, or Saint George with never a dragon left to conquer; a black and white flannel shirt, a blue sash round his waist, a towel in both hands, and his eyes laughing out as he gives the last scrub to his face'.

Taking the cult of the gondolier a stage further, the American painter and author F. Hopkinson Smith fantasised about actually becoming a gondolier: 'When you have spent half the night at the Lido, he swimming at your side, or have rowed all the way to Torcello, or have heard early Mass at San Rosario, away up the Giudecca, he kneeling before you, his hat on the cool pavement next your own, you will begin to lose sight even of the francs, and want to own gondola all yourself, that you may make him guest and thus discharge somewhat the ever-increasing obligation of hospitality under which he places you…He stands with upturned eyes on the graveled walk below. "At what hour will the *Signore* want the Gondola?" You awake from your reverie: Now! as soon as you swallow your coffee. Ten minutes later you bear your weight on Giorgio's bent elbow and step into his boat.'

Hopkinson Smith's gondola fantasy never came true—and as far as can be established, the only man of letters to go beyond the mere seduction or admiration of gondoliers and become one himself, was the English author Frederick Rolfe. In an unlikely but well documented episode, he gave the Cardinal Patriarch of Venice a lift in his boat. The grateful Patriarch amiably appointed him Gondolier in Ordinary, an endorsement that was informal but nevertheless exploited by Rolfe who drummed up a few (not many) fares as a result.

Frederick Rolfe was an eccentric and vigorously homosexual English writer. His satirical and epistolary outpourings were a world away from the delicate meditations of Housman and the romantic effusions of Horatio Brown. He was also known as Baron Corvo and 'Fr. Rolfe'. The title, he claimed, had been bestowed on him by the Duchess Sforza-Cesarini. The 'Fr. Rolfe' could easily have been taken for an abbreviation of 'Frederick', but in reality it was meant to suggest that Rolfe was an ordained Catholic priest: he was not, and despite a promising start, with confirmation by Cardinal Manning, he was expelled from a seminary having been considered lacking in vocation. Rolfe's literary output is largely autobiographical and, given his highly entertaining style, none the worse for that. The highlights of his oeuvre are two novels, *Hadrian VII* and *The Desire and Pursuit of the Whole*. A typical Rolfe plot usually involves a writer, more than slightly irascible, on his uppers through no fault of his own, wronged either by the Church, his friends, his publisher or all of these. There is usually a triumph of some kind, in which the writer gets the better of his enemies through a process of character assassination and thinly disguised emotional blackmail. During the creative process, Rolfe drew heavily on his personal experiences. He spent the last five years of his life in Venice, perpetually broke, endearing himself to a coterie of strapping and willing

Venetian lads but alienating one exasperated expatriate benefactor after another. His wiry form and determined demeanour were a familiar sight on the canals and beaches, his hair cut *en brosse* and dyed, funds permitting, with henna.

Rolfe managed to survive in Venice by what his biographer A.J.A. Symons called, with notable understatement, a 'skilful manipulation of credit and excuses'. The scrounging that Rolfe undertook to keep body and soul together was a drama in itself. Before his eventual ostracism from expatriate society in Venice, he was a regular fixture at Horatio Brown's bachelor parties, where there would be whisky and sandwiches on the sideboard. On one awful occasion he arrived there, hungry, dressed in his last clean item of clothing, a lavender-coloured suit. After what seemed like an interminable conversation with Lord Rosebery, Rolfe gained the sideboard, only to discover that all the sandwiches had been eaten, all the whisky drunk. After a series of ups and downs that found him evicted from his hotel and forced to live in an open boat, he found a safe and agreeable billet— at no less than the Palazzo Mocenigo—with a Dr Van Someren and his wife, Ivy. In addition to bed and board the Van Somerens granted him a small allowance for tobacco and postage stamps, enabling him to indulge two of his favourite pastimes, smoking furiously and writing poisonous or pornographic letters to his enemies or friends in England. For a while all went well, until the ill-starred day he allowed Ivy Van Someren to see the manuscript of his work in progress, *The Desire and Pursuit of the Whole: A Venetian Romance*. She turned the pages of the manuscript in horror for there, in violet ink, in Rolfe's immaculate closely-written hand, were wholly identifiable and painfully acute lampoons of all her circle in Venice—Lady Layard, Canon Wragg, Horatio Brown. Feeling that their hospitality had been roundly abused, the Van Somerens asked Rolfe to leave, and so in March 1910 he was again homeless, wandering the Lido by night.

'Row with pious doctor, and left house on Saturday,' he informed his friend Masson Fox[19]. 'Ate last on Friday evening. Walking all night on Lido beyond Excelsior. Often questioned by Police who are on watch to see that no one evaporates salt from the sea. Say one is writer studying the dawns. So far satisfactory. But the cold is piercing and two nights have made me stiff as a post... Something must be done. But spirits and determination undimmed.'

He persevered in Venice until his death in 1913, lurching from one crisis to the next, spending any money that came his way with a total disregard for his creditors. His most colourful acquisition was a two-masted Vene-

19   Charles Masson Fox.

tian sailing boat that he fitted out with Turkish carpets and leopard-skin trim. After one rare but spectacular windfall he hired no fewer than four gondoliers to ply this boat up and down the Grand Canal, including his favourite oarsman, Baicolo, whom he described as 'the hugest strongest fairest Venetian *toso* you can imagine, a tiger with a simper...'. Venetian fishermen traditionally painted the sails of their vessels and Rolfe, an accomplished painter, tried his hand with spectacular effect. The boat was a familiar sight off the Lido, the mainsail decorated with a life-size nude St George bearing the distinctive white escutcheon splashed with a crimson cross. Beneath this image Rolfe had painted his motto: 'Stand not in my way: nor follow me too far.' His dog often sat in the stern next to a flagstaff flying the Union flag.

VENAL MOONSHINE

Given the tradition of affectionate jokes about reckless Italian drivers it seems appropriate that an important Italian art movement, Filippo Marinetti's Futurism, should have begun with a car crash. His 'Futurist Manifesto' describes how, one evening in Milan in 1911, he and a group of young friends were putting the world to rights. In high-flown language he tells how they 'trampled underfoot native sloth on opulent Persian carpets', 'pushing the outer frontiers of logic, scrawling reams of paper with demented writing.' After a few hours of paperwork the Futurists tire and decide to take their sportscars for a spin—'There were our hot little babes, bonnets ripe for the stroking...'. Marinetti soon took the lead as they raced through the streets, defying the ever-present figure of Death at the crossroads. 'It was a gentrified Reaper that greeted me at every corner, politely beckoning with outstretched hand. There he was again, in the reflections of puddles, enticing me with bedroom eyes and blandishments uttered through creaking jaws.' Inevitably, faced by these distractions, Marinetti ended up head over heels in a ditch. A true Italian motorist, he emerged from the crash unscathed and with a great deal to say, much of it embodied in the Futurist Manifesto, an outpouring that heaps derision on history and sentimentalism, advocating a new masculine age driven by technology, war and speed, 'where the questing, steam-driven liners sniff at the horizon; where barrel-chested locomotives squat snorting on their rails like enormous iron horses festooned with pipes for bridles; where aeroplanes thrust their way across the sky, their propellers mimicking the vigorous flutter of banners, the frenzied applause of crowds.'

This attitude flew in the face of the cautious prescriptions of Ruskin and Henry James—it was clear that Marinetti had no time at all for the 'nostalgic' view of Venice that had flourished in the 19th century. In 1910 he wrote a rousing call to arms, *Contro Venezia passatista*, flinging thousands of copies from the Campanile of San Marco in a well-calculated publicity stunt that gained the young Futurists more than passing notice:

Away with you, venerable old Venice, spent and ruined by voluptuousness. We loved one another well enough, while the nostalgic dream lasted, but now it's rejection time. To hell with that Venice mooned over by tourists! Damn that forgers' bazaar, that magnet for snobs and imbeciles, that four-poster smashed in by caravans-full of shaggers, that jewel-encrusted girdle for cosmopolitan old sluts, that Grand Privy of traditionalism. Let us cleanse and cauterise this putrescent city, this festering bubo of the past. Let us bring back to life and re-enoble the Venetians themselves, busting up their nasty, furtive little businesses. Let us prepare for the birth of an industrial and military might in Venice that'll ravish that great Italian lake, the Adriatic, once and for all. There's no time to lose. Fill in all the stinking little canals with the rubble of those crumbling, leprous palaces. Burn all the gondolas, those rocking chairs for cretins. Raise up to high heaven a glorious symmetry of iron bridges, topped by a great canopy of smoke from the factories. What a backlash *that* would be at the sagging curves of the miserable old buildings! And yes, may it come! The reign of Divine Electric Light, that will liberate Venice once and for all from the venal moonshine that illuminates all those 'furnished apartments'![20]

The wilder extremes of Marinetti's vision never caught on. Italians, particularly the shrewd Venetians, were too cautious to embrace wholesale cultural desecration of the kind advocated by Marinetti. Nevertheless, there was a definite swing towards technological progress, and for a while a very real threat that the 'glorious symmetry of metal bridges' might become a reality. Eugenio Miozzi, the architect of the Ponte della Libertà that connects Venice to the mainland, had prepared elaborate proposals for the bridging of the entire lagoon. If he had had his way, all of the major islands, including the

20   Translations from Marinetti by RS.

Lido, would have been interconnected by road and rail bridges. There was a fierce backlash against these proposals led by a group of people from various quarters at home and abroad, collectively known as '*antipontisti*'. Anyone to this day who is against bridges of the kind proposed by Miozzi is known as an *antipontista*.

There were, meanwhile, those who were determined at all costs to commercialise what Marinetti had unwittingly identified as Venice's most bankable commodity, 'Venal Moonshine'. This could not be bottled and sold, but its gleam could certainly be intensified and focused so as to lure the new money of Europe to the economically ailing Serenissima. The Lido, as yet undeveloped in any coherent sense, despite the foundation of the bathing establishments, was an ideal place to start a new, upmarket tourist industry that would resurrect the fortunes of Venice and restore something of the economic autonomy it had enjoyed in the high days of the Republic.

The visionaries of the new Lido were the entrepreneur Nicolò Spada and politician-tycoon Count Giuseppe di Volpi Misurata. Spada, the founder of the Italian hotel group CIGA[21], was the first to seize the initiative, unifying and giving shape to the somewhat muddled entrepreneurial activity that had taken place on the Lido since the foundation of the *stabilimenti*. He

21   Compagnia Italiana Grandi Alberghi.

swept away the bureaucracy and debate that had frustrated any major development for decades. Land that had previously been jealously guarded by the Italian military was quietly bought up by Spada's consortium. Any objections that more conservative Venetians might pose to the developments were countered with carefully thought-out and sensitive suggestions as to planning. Questions as to what could and couldn't be built on the precious shoreline were carefully addressed. When open consultation failed, the payment of handsome incentives ensured that any pedantic obstacles to the new vision were put to one side. By 1908, Spada had ineradicably stamped the identity of CIGA on the Lido: the Grand Hotel Excelsior and the Grand Hotel des Bains had been completed and there followed a brisk spate of commercial and residential development on the Lido that has continued, with occasional doldrums, to the present day.

The success of the great hotels brought about a fresh wave of development throughout the early 20th century. Whilst architects like Giovanni Sardi were free from the draconian constraints to which they would have been subjected while working on the Grand Canal, the authorities nevertheless kept a close eye on new buildings. For the most part, the new build on the Lido was very 'safe', a mixture of predictable neo-Gothic seasoned with an occasional reference to Art Nouveau. But amid the respectable and quite pretty villas there are a few outstanding examples of what in Italy is misleading called the 'Liberty' style. The most notable is the Villino Monplaisir on the corner of Via Lepanto and the Gran Viale. Designed by Guido Costante Sullam and completed in 1906 for Spada, it is a truly original work, devoid of any theme-park *venezianismo* and rich in references to some of the great contemporary masters that Sullam admired, among these Baron Horta and Hoffmann. An active and respected member of the Jewish community in Venice, Sullam designed the entrance to the Modern Jewish Cemetery in Via Cipro and several tombs, notably those of the Levi family and of Amedeo Errer. He brought the same dignified and eclectic lightness of touch to funerary art as he did to the design of *villini*. A later masterpiece, designed by Brenno del Giudice and completed in 1927, is the so-called House of the Pharmacist in Via Sandro Gallo. Halfway down the Gran Viale is the Grande Albergo Hungaria Ausonia, built by Nicolò Piamonte in 1905–08, its towering elevations clad in luxurious ceramic tiles by Luigi Fabris.

The Grand Hotel Excelsior and the Grand Hotel des Bains were completed in 1908 and 1909 respectively. Giovanni Sardi's Excelsior is a bright, airy Veneto-Byzantine-Moorish extravaganza. Unlike the Hotel des Bains, which stands on the west side of the Lungomare Guglielmo Marconi, the Excelsior stands directly on the beach, which has always lent it a slightly more festive and unbuttoned ambience. First-time visitors to the

Excelsior—both before and after the recent refurbishment—are always struck by the exuberant sense of space, the sheer scale of the building inside and out, a grandeur as much in evidence in the suites as in the public spaces. This owes much to the unique collaboration between the client, Spada, and his chosen architect Giovanni Sardi, a fellow Venetian who had made his name with the unimpeachable if slightly unambitious neo-Gothic Bauer-Grünwald Hotel on the Grand Canal.

The two men enjoyed a close working relationship and for both of them the Excelsior project turned out to be ideal, uninhibited by questions of cost (the budget was seemingly unlimited) and stimulated by compatible objectives. Spada wanted the building to be something rather more than a straightforward, typically Venetian, Gothic or Classical pastiche; Sardi wanted to break free from the constraints that had been imposed on him in the Bauer-Grünwald project, where the building had had to fit in with its revered neighbours on the Grand Canal. The finished hotel on the Lido, they agreed, should be unmistakably Venetian in feel, yet sufficiently cosmopolitan to please its international clientèle. It should have all the familiar components of luxury that guests would have enjoyed in the hotels of Cairo, Paris, Baden-Baden and Monte Carlo, but there should also be an extra *brivido*, an element of surprise that would make the Excelsior an overnight name and draw in the international set. Furthermore, the hotel should be fun and uplifting, its guests exchanging their responsibilities for an intense interlude of masterfully managed hedonism not available to them in the elegant though somewhat forbidding European spas and sanatoria. The resulting confection, a resounding success for both Spada and Sardi, was completed in a little under 18 months. It opened in July 1908 with a beach party at which there were upwards of 3,000 guests. The greatly admired interior was decorated by a number of well-known designers, the most prominent being Mariano Fortuny[22] who floated around Venice, Ugo Ojetti tells us, '…simple and sober as an anchorite. Dressed in simple clothes even in the icy *bora*, always of the same colour and material, a cloak of black cloth, a suit of dark blue serge, a white silk tie, soft black hat, low patent-leather shoes or red braided-leather sandals'. Fortuny designed the Gaming Room, hanging it with soft fabrics to create an impression of warmth and movement, an idea he repeated the Spanish pavilion of the Venice Biennale in 1924. Interior decorators today may profit from Ojetti's reminder that when Fortuny did 'pink' it was not the pink of other men, but a pink 'stolen by his sylph from a rising moon.'

The Grand Hotel des Bains, designed by Francesco Marsich, is a comparatively restrained classical build-

---

22   Mariano Fortuny (1871–1949), Spanish-born couturier and textile designer whose family moved to Venice in 1889.

ing, a discreet rather than a flamboyant venue, attract-
ing a refined clientèle that included Thomas Mann
and, later, Marlene Dietrich[23]. Whilst the Excelsior in-
tentionally had the air of the grand fleshpots of Cairo,
Alexandria and Istanbul, the Hotel des Bains recalled
the valetudinarian hush of the great luxury spas and
sanatoria of Baden Baden and Zurich. It quickly became
the haunt of cosmopolitan old money, or at any rate a
slightly older species of new money, though there were,
among the guests, those who led a decidedly precarious
existence and were often short of cash. One such was
the ballet impresario Serge Diaghilev, who holidayed on
the Lido for many years, discreetly supported by rich
friends when funds were low.

He held court annually, attended by a close inner circle of colleagues and friends that included Serge Lifar,
Boris Kochno and Coco Chanel. From time to time visitors paid homage, among them Isadora Duncan, who
was photographed by her brother Raymond pirouetting
along the rainswept beach. The poet Carl Sandburg, in
his poem 'Isadora Duncan' sums up the spirit of her art
very aptly. In the poem, he has the dancer herself celebrate her credo: 'I dance what I am', expressing in dance

---

23   In September 1937 a somewhat disconsolate Marlene Dietrich, recov-
ering from the recent Korda flop *Knight Without Armour*, was sitting in the
Hotel des Bains with Josef von Sternberg. Erich Maria Remarque, the author
of *All Quiet on the Western Front*, came over and asked her to dance. Subsequently, their brief but intense affair restored her confidence.

the element or concept to which she feels attuned at any given moment: sea, sun, moon, tears, sin, prayer, pain. Isadora organised a memorable outing in which she, Diaghilev and Lifar visited the exotic Marchesa Casati at Palazzo Venier dei Leoni[24]. She danced with Lifar, a fascinating union of two very different disciplines. The Marchesa, with flame-red hair, alabster-white face and enormous dark eyes, looked on, wearing a Leon Bakst frock, all peacock feathers and jewels, accompanied by her two pet cheetahs, safely restrained on their diamond-encrusted leashes.

In September 1911, Diaghilev was visited at the Hotel des Bains by Igor Stravinsky who played to him, on the ballroom piano, the first draft of the 'Danse des Adolescentes' from *The Rite of Spring*. Diaghilev, who always kept an eye and ear on the attention span of an audience, cut in while Stravinsky was in full flow. 'How long does this last?' he asked. Stravinsky replied sharply, 'As long as it lasts…' It certainly didn't go down too well at the first performance, as Stravinsky himself was the first to admit[25]. From the opening bars onwards there were rumblings of disapproval, but it was the appearance of the *Adolescentes*, described damningly by Stravinsky as 'knock-kneed and long-braided Lolitas', that sealed the production's fate once and for all. There were cries of

24   One of the Marchesa's homes in Italy, later bought by Peggy Guggenheim and now the home of the Guggenheim Museum.
25   See W. Austin, *Music in the Twentieth Century* (New York, 1966, p. 196).

'Shame!'—and the composer stormed out of the audi-
torium, slamming the stage door nearest the orchestra
pit in his fury.

In 1929, when Diaghilev died in his darkened room in
the des Bains, the faithful Chanel dealt with the unpaid
bills and organised his funeral at San Michele. Chanel, a
shrewd self-educator who had surrounded herself with
a serviceable constellation of civilised or rich men, was
a regular visitor to the Lido and a committed lover of
Venice. There is an amusing account of her Venetian
voyage of cultural discovery, not to mention self-dis-
covery, in Edmonde Charles-Roux's biography, where
Chanel is depicted as having to make that agonising
choice, faced by so many citizens of the *demi-monde*,
between 'culture' and 'life'. In the end, Charles-Roux
tells us, she chose life, abandoning Venice's museums
and churches in favour of days spent larking about on
the beach with Serge Lifar, evenings spent in Harry's Bar
and long trips with her lover 'Bendor', the 2nd Duke
of Westminster. Nevertheless, the practical *couturière* in
Chanel was never far from the surface, whatever diversions were on offer. Nowhere did her down-to-earth ef-
ficiency shine more brightly than at Diaghilev's funeral,
which she volunteered to organise and pay for, much
to the relief of her friend Misia Sert, who was becoming increasingly hysterical at the prospect of having to
sell a diamond necklace in order to mollify the under-
taker. Breezing back into Venice aboard the Duke of

Westminster's yacht, *Flying Cloud*, Chanel immediately took charge of the arrangements. Three gondolas departed from the Lido at dawn, bound for the cemetery of San Michele, bearing Diaghilev and his four mourners: Misia and Chanel, Boris Kochno and Serge Lifar. By the time they arrived, Kochno and Lifar had decided to make the final journey to the tomb on their knees, a piece of choreography that Chanel peremptorily ruled out. 'No more of that nonsense if you please!'—though she was unable to restrain Lifar from leaping into the open grave, a *grand pas* he presumably executed with wholly characteristic agility and passion.

Chanel had her detractors, among them the Russian-American songwriter and composer Vernon Duke, who memorably described her, in his memoir *Passport to Paris*, as looking like a 'jockey in drag'. He brings to life the atmosphere of post-Diaghilev Venice, where the shambolic days of the old high style still lingered on. He recalls going to tea with Elizabeth Chavchavadze in the Palazzo Polignac, swimming at the Lido with her daughter, hearing Shostakovich's *Lady Macbeth of Mzensk* 'energetically booed' at the Fenice, visiting a venerable old Russian countess and her four large, unkempt, poodles.

The des Bains was an entirely appropriate retreat for an habitually anguished soul like Thomas Mann, who used it as the setting for his famous novella, *Death in Venice*, which was subsequently made into a film by Luchino Visconti. In the novella, Mann recreates the quietly sophisticated, ultra-cosmopolitan atmosphere of the hotel. Many languages are spoken, all of them in subdued, carefully modulated tones. A troubled middle-aged author, Gustav von Aschenbach, arrives in Venice for a solitary and soul-searching stay at the hotel. He has a series of disturbing encounters—one with a sinister red-haired man and another with a gondolier—all of which convincingly point towards latent and unfulfilled homosexuality. He develops an obsession for Tadzio, a beautiful and aristocratic Polish adolescent who is staying at the hotel with his family. He watches, enchanted, as the boy sports on the beach or glides around the lobby in his immaculate sailor suit. He prolongs his trip, even when he learns that Venice is in the throes of a serious cholera epidemic, hitherto hushed up by the authorities. He knows he ought to warn Tadzio's family about the epidemic, but he is scared that if he does, Tadzio will be taken away and he will never see him again. The Polish family notice the increasing intensity with which von Aschenbach stares at Tadzio and they warn the boy to steer clear of the unbalanced stranger. Von Aschenbach visits a barber in an attempt to roll back the years and recapture his youth, an adventure that results in a distinctly unwholesome new look featuring dyed hair and grotesquely applied rouge. Thus improved, he follows Tadzio through the streets of Venice one morning but eventually loses sight of him. Resting at a small *trattoria*, he contemplates the intricacies of Platonic love while ill-advisedly tucking into a plate of over-ripe and unhygienically prepared strawberries. The virus takes hold. Back at the Lido, he learns that Tadzio and his family are about to leave. The last von Aschenbach sees of him is on the beach. Slumped in his deckchair, he sees Tadzio fight with another lad, Jasiu. After the fight Tadzio seems to turn and beckon to his admirer. Von Aschenbach attempts to rise and go to him, but falls back into the chair, dead.

The idea for the story came to Thomas Mann on a family holiday to Venice in 1911. His wife Katia clearly remembered the circumstances, later describing the Polish family in detail, the somewhat severely dressed girls in stark contrast to the strikingly beautiful thirteen-year-old boy in his open-collared sailor suit. Katia conceded that her husband watched the boy and his friends playing on the beach but rejected the idea that he might have pursued him across Venice, as von Aschenbach does with Tadzio in the novella. An interesting cameo role in the real-life Death in Venice saga, as related by Katia, is that played by Mann's father-in-law, Privy Counsellor Friedburg, a well-known and straight-laced professor of canon law at Leipzig. 'What a story!' he said, outraged by the book, 'And he a *family* man!'

Von Aschenbach is said to be based in part on Gustav Mahler, whose music Visconti used in the film, and in part on the homosexual German romantic poet August von Platen-Hallermünde. Some say the red-haired man represents the ancient god Silenus, bent on pursuing the hero and bringing about his destruction. It is certainly true that a heady air of paganism and tortured classical learning pervades the *haut-bourgeois* opulence of the setting.

Visconti's film, *Morte a Venezia*, is a great masterpiece. Its beauties have been roundly praised. Dirk Bogarde, who gives a memorable performance as von Aschenbach, dye trickling down his pansticked and rouge-ravaged face in the blazing heat, recounts several amusing *Morte a Venezia* stories in his memoirs. In one volume, *An Orderly Man*, he reveals that Warner Brothers were on the brink of withdrawing the film for fear it might upset the moral majority in the USA. Luckily, a gala première in London, attended by the Queen and held in aid of various restoration projects in Venice, gave the film the cachet of respectability it needed and worldwide distribution went ahead. The good-looking and engagingly down-to-earth Tadzio, Björn Andrésen, celebrated the release by buying himself a new motorcycle. A lesser-sung hero of the Visconti triumph is the great Italian cinematographer Pasqualino de Santis, who met his director's grandiose ambitions in high style. In the opening sequence de Santis's camera cruises slowly and luxuriously along the Lido in a continuous and miraculously unbroken shot, taking in hundreds of beautifully turned-out holidaymakers. He achieved the extraordinarily vivid and shimmering play of light by stretching enormous sheets and sails all along the beach to filter, focus and intensify the sun. It is easy, when watching the film, to align oneself with Mann who, long after his inspired visit to Venice in 1911, wrote to his children, Klaus and Erika, who were visiting the city, saying that he was with them in spirit, knowing that they were 'leading that unique life between the warm sea in the morning and the "ambiguous" city in the afternoon.'

The Hotel des Bains is being redeveloped as I write this, part of a huge project largely underwritten by EST Capital in partnership with the Comune di Venezia. Rumours in the British press that it was under threat of permanent closure are without foundation and it will reopen as a smaller but no less luxurious hotel, a sizeable proportion of the old space reincarnated as luxury apartments, a sensible way of refiltering the venal moonshine without compromising historical integrity. There has been much gleefully morbid gossip about committee-driven feasibility studies of the past that preceded the involvement of EST. For example, there was the question of the grand old mirrors in the des Bains ballroom that in their time had reflected Coco Chanel and Isadora Duncan, Stravinsky and Diaghilev. It had been suggested that the glass in these mirrors be replaced because it was 'old, rotten and smoky'. A new hotel needs new glazing throughout, ran the thinking, so the old glass would have to go. The proposal was seconded by a specialist in the Italian equivalent of Health and Safety, who expatiated on the dangers of even *looking* at antique mirrors. You might lose your footing, he claimed, or worse.

None of this will happen—the reglazing proposal was overruled, because of the Italian genius for the eleventh-hour ruling out of destructive errors of taste such as these. Some years ago at the Excelsior, for example, there was a terrifying interlude during which the grand ballroom was at risk, not from health and safety fanatics but from a marketing consultant specialising in 'best practice' and 'facilities management'. The ballroom, known as the Sala degli Stucchi because of its exquisitely elaborate stucco cornices and cupids, was to have been carved up into a series of 'cost-effective' conference spaces. Any inconveniently placed putti were to be hacked off to make way for 'versatile' room-divider fixings. The massive Umberto Bellotto chandeliers that for a century had softened and dappled the silk and velvets of Fortuny, Chanel and Balenciaga gowns were to be wrenched out and replaced with 'site-specific' lighting. 'They would have to kill me first,' said a well known local man possessed of considerable power and influence—and he meant it. And so the Sala degli Stucchi is safe. It is possible, in peaceful late August, to wander into the vast space unchallenged and sit alone beneath the chandeliers and meditate, or even tap away at a laptop as I did, writing these very words.

HARDER, FASTER...

On the northern tip of the Lido, past the Jewish Cemetery and near the Caserma Pepe barracks, stands the Aeroporto Nicelli, the Art Deco home of the flying club[26] and named after the Venetian air ace Giovanni Nicelli, who claimed eight kills in the First World War. The first, very simple, airstrip was laid down as early as 1909 when the Italian army began to operate an internal postal service. 1912 saw the first glimmers of characteristic Venetian showmanship when crowds gathered in San Marco to watch the pilot Umberto Cagno make the first ever flight over Venice. The airport came into its own in the First World War when there was a serious danger that the city would be bombed by Austria.

The threat of aerial bombardment had darkened the skies of Venice in the past, during the Venetian uprising against Austria under Daniele Manin. In those days there had been a frightening but ultimately shambolic attempt at bombardment using balloons, mastermind-

26   More adventurous visitors can indulge in parachuting (*paracadutismo*) by arrangement with the Aeroclub. The Nicelli website provides an interesting overview of the airport's history (www.aeroportonicelli.it). As the result of a collaboration between the Italian engineer Renato Morandi and Hugo Junkers, the German aeronautical designer and manufacturer, the Lido was for a time the Italian home of Transadriatica, a joint venture that ran commercial flights, the first of their kind, from Venice (departing from Nicelli) to Vienna.

ed by a Lieutenant Paulizza of the Austrian army, in peacetime an admirer of Effie Ruskin. Now, the prospects were much more serious and Venice prepared to defend herself from air attack.

Since there was only a skeleton air squadron available on the nearby island of Le Vignole, an arrangement was quickly made to station French reinforcements on the Lido. The resulting allied air initiative has taken its place in Venetian history, thanks in large measure to one of the leading participants, Gabriele d'Annunzio.

D'Annunzio was a poet, an unusually resourceful one, cast in the Byronic mould of cultivated *machismo*. Upon the outbreak of the First World War he was 51, and by then a revered if somewhat louche literary figure with a string of novels, poems, plays and mistresses to his credit. As such, he proved a tremendous asset to the newly-formed Italian airforce and cast himself energetically in the role of fearless airman. He moved from the Casa Rossetta, his lair on the Grand Canal, to comparatively spartan lodgings on the Lido at No. 24 Via Lepanto. A routine cockpit accident had left him with a dashing eye-patch and he wisely made no effort to correct the widespread assumption that this was a battle scar won in some dangerous exploit. The small deception was overlooked in the face of his unlimited energy and charisma, especially by the French allies. Already a literary hero in France, he was tremendously popular with the French officers, who in turn were warmly welcomed by the Venetians. The French had brought with them a four-strong brigade of chefs and their HQ at the Albergo Paradiso on the Lido quickly became the focus of welcome social activity that blunted the tedium of life at war. D'Annunzio held court as host and made sure that the allied unit was cheered along by a procession of distinguished visitors. These included the writer Louis-Ferdinand Céline, the Prince of Wales (later Edward VIII) and the Baronessa Nicola Winspeare Guicciardi.

Among his brother Italians d'Annunzio cleverly boosted morale by renaming the Italian 87th Air Squadron the Squadron of St Mark, thus giving it a stirring Venetian identity of its own. In time the 87th, under d'Annunzio's leadership, came to be known simply but effectively as 'La Serenissima'. Its proudest moment—perhaps, an ultimate example of what the pen can achieve without the assistance of the sword—was the 'bombing' of Vienna in August 1918. In this sortie, celebrated in Italian airforce lore as the *Volo su Vienna*, no bombs were dropped. Instead, nine aeroplanes from La Serenissima dropped over 50,000 flyers, written by d'Annunzio himself and printed in the Italian national colours of red, white and green, heralding the end of German domination in Austria. No matter that the war was all but over—the bombardment was seen by Italians as a consummate act of heroism. In later wars it was always held up as the first successful dissemination of printed propaganda by aerial bombardment.

While d'Annunzio played his part as an airman, there were other developments in the Lido's war effort. The Hotel des Bains was transformed into a temporary home for child refugees. According to the official history of the American Red Cross in Italy[27], the children could not have had a more agreeable billet. The ballroom where Stravinsky had sparred with Diaghilev was turned into a dormitory, with rows of dainty blue and white beds. The shaded terrace where Thomas Mann had sat in inspired contemplation became a makeshift refectory. The children were allowed to use the beach and to play in the pinewoods, careful supervision preventing them from becoming stuck in the barbed wire entanglements. They wore brightly-coloured aprons, made by soldier's wives and embroidered with a red cross and the letters CRA (Croce Rossa Americana). There were toys, bathing costumes, games and delicious food, the des Bains kitchen having been completely rebuilt after fire damage early on in the war. The colony was presided over by firm but kindly black-robed nuns and Red Cross nurses drafted in from Venice and as far afield as Rome.

By the end of the war, Venetians were all too ready to return to their glamorous role as hosts to the rich tourists of America and Europe. Count Giuseppe di Volpi Misurata built on Spada's pre-war legacy, actively en-

27   *The Story of the American Red Cross in Italy*, Charles M. Bakewell, 1920.

couraging upmarket tourism by, amongst other things, ensuring that the Schneider Trophy air race took place at the Lido every three years. This, together with other attractions he sponsored, such as the international motor-boat races and the Casino, kept the Lido on the map as an international resort.

The Schneider Trophy, a glamorous affair, drew in a new breed of rich English, French and American speed kings and queens, set on thrashing their cars, boats and planes harder, faster and for longer than their rivals. The bittersweet scent of *Adieu Sagesse* on the terrace of the Excelsior and the strains of Belle Epoque melody in the ballroom of the Hotel des Bains were replaced by the aphrodisiac whiff of *benzina* and the libido-stirring roar of Rolls Royce engines. The Excelsior marked the finishing post of the air race, which comprised a circuit of the Lido from San Nicolò to Alberoni and back. A report of the 1927 Schneider Trophy race, won for Britain by Flt Lt Sidney Webster of the RAF, gives a good idea of the atmosphere[28]. 'These three whirled, as it were, around the clock in most thrilling fashion. On the longest side of the triangular course, Webster dashed in pursuit of Guazetti. For one breathless moment the machines were level, and in the next the royal blue of the British machine was seen a quarter of a mile ahead of the blood red Italian, proving that the British engines

28   *Evening Post*, 27th September 1927.

were immeasurably the faster. Webster, who is stockily built, stepped nonchalantly from his machine, showing no signs of the ordeal through which he had passed. He quietly remarked, "I am so jolly glad I won for Britain. She is going to celebrate. So shall I.'"

The Lido was now popular with a younger breed of Americans, few if any of them resembling Henry James. In June 1921 a group of Harvard men gathered on the terrace of the *stabilimento* and sang a medley of university favourites including 'Harvardiana' and 'Onward, Crimson!' When suitably warmed up, they give a rousing performance of the *Inno di Mameli* with, according to the *Gazzettino*, great 'clarity of accent and martial intonation'. 'The twenties were the years of postwar American gaiety in Europe,' wrote Margaret Case in her memoir, *Take Them Up Tenderly*, 'and the Cole Porters were happily involved with the shining fleet of vicomtes, contessas, princes incognito, and rich Americans that swept from Paris to London, to the Lido, to the Riviera, with Elsa Maxwell as the tireless tugboat that pulled them forever onward.'

Elsa Maxwell (1883–1963) was an American gossip columnist, songwriter and professional hostess who had allegedly been 'hired'—it was never clear exactly by whom—to help stimulate the social life of Venice in the 1920s. She was a regular and resourceful partygiver and it seems likely that the terms of her 'contract' amounted to an unspoken agreement with Volpi and his colleagues at CIGA that she would enjoy substantial discounts in return for giving amusing parties for carefully-chosen guests, buoying up the social whirl and making sure all notable events were reported in her columns. A short, stout, unprepossessing woman, she was capable of great ruthlessness but had a pronounced streak of vulnerability. Duff Cooper, who attended several of her parties in Venice, recalled an occasion when she failed to deliver, leaving over a hundred guests stranded and without supper. That night, she was eventually found in bed in her tiny apartment, too scared to face the music. She had a keen eye for the main chance, though. Once, on a visit to the indiscriminately generous Barbara Hutton, she casually admired a jewelled cigarette case worth about $30,000. 'Have it,' said Hutton. 'Thank you,' said Maxwell, quietly and quickly slipping it into her handbag[29].

Between 1923 and 1927 the Cole Porters came every summer to Venice where they gave a series of elaborate parties, some staged on an enormous float, permanently moored in the lagoon and known by Venetians as *l'arca di Noe*, 'Noah's Ark'. These excesses were greeted with disgust by Diaghilev, who complained strenuously about the jazz, the 'negroes' and the nightclub. In addition, he cannot have been anything but dismayed

29   For the source of this and other instances of how the Woolworth heiress was exploited by unscrupulous hangers-on, see *Million Dollar Baby: an Intimate Portrait of Barbara Hutton* by Philip van Rensselaer.

by another philistine raid on the Ballet Russes' citadel, Porter's brief but intense affair with the dancer and librettist Boris Kochno. Despite Diaghilev's protestations, the revellers voted with their feet and Cole Porter's elaborately orchestrated *tumulte noir* was there to stay: he shipped in the all-black Leslie Hutchinson jazz orchestra to perform at Chez Vous; the legendary black singer Bricktop sang at Jane di San Faustino's charity gala in 1926; chorus lines of flappers were taught the Charleston on the Lido beach. Some of the more *outré* fringe performances that took place during Porter's reign included a ukulele routine by an Indian nobleman, Prince Jit of Kapurthala, and an appearance by the short, stout and irrepressible Elsa Maxwell, wearing a blonde wig and a short, tight skirt, singing 'I'm a little old Lido lady'. As to Porter's patronage of gondoliers, it would have rendered gondola-chasers like Symonds and Brown speechless, for he routinely employed no fewer than fifty gondoliers to act as footmen at his parties in the Ca'Rezzonico. In a hothouse such as this, it was only a question of time before 'Lido' was rhymed with 'libido'. Porter duly obliged, improvising a lewd stanza touching on a supposed liaison between the 'leader of the Big-Time Band' and the well-known French author George Sand.

The Thirties saw no slackening of tone or pace in Lido life. *L'Officiel de la mode*, a *Hello!* of its day, made intoxicating reading for lovers of high society gossip.

Even today, though many of the participants are half or wholly forgotten, a recital of their sonorous names is enough to conjure a sense of the past, an hypnotic litany of abandon, privilege and luxury: Prince Alexis Mdivani sets off for the Lido in his speedboat, the *Ali Baba*. There he meets the Prince of Piedmont, heir to the Italian throne, on the Excelsior beach. Nearby sits Jimmy Walker, the former mayor of New York, meditating on the vicissitudes of politics. Serge Lifar basks in the sun while an energetic Stanislas de la Rochefoucauld gives a rowing lesson to the Countess of Beauchamp. In the middle distance Princess Adelaide of Savoy perches on a raft, chatting to the Prince of Bavaria while their companion, President Roosevelt's son James, flings himself into the Adriatic. Even the hard-working and distinguished Romanian statesman Titulescu confesses to *L'Officiel* that he can't live long without returning to the Lido. Sacha Guitry, having a few hours to kill between trains, shows Jacqueline Delubac the Doge's Palace before setting off to the Lido for tea. The French Ambassador tops up his tan, comparing notes with Lady Latham and George V's nephew, the Earl of Cambridge. Count Volpi whisks Principessa Ruspoli back to his *palazzo* by boat, while the Princesse de Polignac warmly welcomes her friend Jean de Castellane. Barbara Hutton, the Woolworth heiress and now Princess Mdivani, rejoins her husband on the beach having spent the day running riot with an open chequebook among the coral merchants and glass-makers of Murano.

Volpi's most enduring legacy to Venice and the Lido—and one in which the Excelsior played a central part—was his inspired decision, in 1932, to hold an international exhibition of film in Venice as part of the already well established Biennale. The Venice Biennale, an international arts festival, had been founded in 1885 and had gone from strength to strength, largely as a result of the 'national pavilions' that were built in the Giardini di Castello from 1907 onwards, at the outset of the building and design boom in Venice. By the Thirties, most European countries, and the United States, had their own pavilions and therefore a tangible territorial stake in the Biennale. They exhibited their art in an atmosphere of, in the main, stimulating and amicable competition. With characteristic foresight, Volpi responded to the boom in the motion picture industry following the advent of the 'talkies', adding a cinematic wing to the festival that would draw in a fresh wave of visitors to the city. As a minister in Mussolini's government and as a powerful businessman in his own right, Volpi dismissed bureaucratic objections even more aggressively than Spada had done in the early days of the CIGA developments. All red tape was swiftly cut and the first 'Esposizione Internazionale d'Arte Cinematografica', the Venice Film Festival, took place in 1932 on the terrace of the Excelsior. It was the first festival of its kind, Cannes being a junior late-comer in 1946.

The beach-side location was a popular choice and the first screenings were a huge success. Though the festival later moved to the Palazzo del Cinema, a large and severe Rationalist building by Eugenio Miozzi, the Excelsior has remained the favoured hang-out of stars, directors and their entourages. As time went by, the festival brought about a perceptible and entirely ap-propriate change of atmosphere in the hotel, intensify-ing the air of light-hearted and luxurious hedonism it had cultivated since 1908. It became, to use a cine-matic term, decidedly *telefono bianco* in feel, the phrase *telefono bianco* ('white telephone') being an affectionate way of referring to the crop of amusing post-war Ital-ian films that celebrated love and life against carefree, luxurious and beautifully-appointed backdrops. White telephones, deep carpets, beautiful clothes and leop-ardskin rugs were the order of the day in these films, which many Italians saw as a preferable alternative to the offerings of Vittorio de Sica (*Bicycle Thieves*) and other exponents of the new, uncompromising realism.

Winston Churchill was devoted to the Excelsior and was a great fan of the festival. John Julius Norwich re-calls[30] how, as a boy, he was taken to a festival screening. He sat next to Churchill, who was deeply engrossed in

30   In conversation with the author.

a film about gypsies, with not a single white telephone to be seen. One of Churchill's idiosyncrasies was a tendency to talk incessantly during films, occasionally to companions but mostly to himself, delivering an oratorically flawless running commentary on the triumphs and tribulations of the characters. 'Poor people…' he murmured with exquisite timing, as the camera panned in on the squalor of the gypsy encampment. 'Poor, *poor* people…' Later in the film, one of the hotter-blooded gypsies flew into a temper and strangled his sweetheart to death. 'Jealousy,' said Churchill with conviction. 'Jealousy…'—he lowered his voice for effect—'…the *basest* of human instincts…'.

The first serious scandal—and it did the festival no harm—was the furore following the screening in 1933 of the Czech director Gustav Machatý's film *Ekstase*, 'Ecstasy'. The film starred Hedy Lamarr, then known as Hedy Kiesler, a newcomer to the profession and an attractive ingénue, yet to blossom into the feisty vamp of the 1940s. She starred in *Ekstase* as Eva Hermann, a simmering young beauty who marries a pleasant but irretrievably desiccated older man. On their wedding night, minutely and embarrassingly observed by Machatý, the groom fails to consummate the marriage. The disappointed Eva becomes increasingly frustrated, nowhere less so than on their honeymoon at a mountain resort, where she is tormented by the sight of hundreds of loving couples either urgently petting in the alpine

sunshine or gazing at one another in glueily sated fulfil-
ment. One day, weeks into the marriage, she medita-
tively bathes naked in a woodland stream, deploring
her passionless existence. Fortuitously, her horse bolts
and her ultimate deliverance arrives in the shape of
Adam, a strapping if somewhat one-dimensional young
engineer who helps her recapture the animal, falling in
love with her along the way. One evening, having been
caught in a violent storm, the pair make their way to
Adam's cottage where they strip off and make love. At
this point Machatý chose to orchestrate the first ever
on-screen orgasm, filming a tight close-up of Lamarr's
face while simultaneously, off camera, pricking her but-
tocks with a safety pin. The resultant grimaces were sufficiently convincing to shock the authorities, so much
so that the film was condemned by the Patriarch of Venice and listed by the Catholic Church as an unwholesome and immoral work of art.

Offscreen, there was a decided downturn in moral
standards among rich tourists in Venice. For a small
but prominent British clique, September 1932 was, in
the words of Diana Mosley's biographer Ann de Courcy,
'eventful in the annals of the Lido'. The decorum that
had characterised Lido life before the First World War,
when Thomas Mann had stayed at the Hotel des Bains,
was now a quaint memory. This was an unbuttoned
Lido, a Lido of loose beach pyjamas designed by Carl
Novitsky, of exuberantly kicked-off espadrilles, long,

bibulous luncheons and dinners at Chez Vous, picnics outside the Excelsior's beach cabins and breathless fornication inside them. This was the perfect backdrop for Oswald Mosley, lotos-eating after a strenuous, eventful and unsuccessful year in politics, his Fascist New Party having been conclusively trounced in the General Election of 1931. Since the British Union of Fascists, to be launched in earnest in October 1932, was still at the planning stage, September was free for Mosley's annual visit to the Lido, where he was able to set politics aside and focus intensively on an adulterous affair with his future wife Diana, the most beautiful of the Mitford sisters, at that point still married to Bryan Guinness.

Mosley, 'Tom' to his friends, was a good organiser. He let no opportunity for an assignation slip by, remaining resolutely undeterred by the presence on the Lido of his wife Cimmie and of Diana's husband, Bryan. 'I shall need your room tonight between midnight and 4am,' he instructed Bob Boothby, one of the circle. 'But Tom, where shall I sleep?' complained Boothby. 'On the beach, Bob,' came the resolute answer. Deprived of his room, Boothby slept in Mosley's beach cabin. Other sideshows of the season included a fight, on the beach, between Winston Churchill's son Randolph and Brendan Bracken, in which Randolph snapped Brendan's spectacles in two and cast them into the Adriatic. The incident was triggered by Randolph's sarcastic reference to Brendan as his 'dear brother', an allusion to the scandalous rumours that Bracken was the illegitimate son of Churchill. Randolph, having thus disposed of Brendan's spectacles, spent the rest of his time in singleminded pursuit of the Austrian-born dancer Tilly Losch. Tilly's husband meanwhile, the British Surrealist poet Edward James, consoled himself with a series of unsuccessful attempts to seduce Serge Lifar, a regular basker on the sands. In the final analysis, then, it cannot be said that the British had failed to hold their own in this enduringly cosmopolitan and very competitive playground.[31] Oswald Mosley, in his autobiography *My Life*, muses eloquently on the Lido high life of the period, comparing the many British, continental and American society hostesses he knew. His style is elegant, light and good-humoured, surprisingly at variance with the Valentino-in-knuckledusters image inevitably conferred on him by posterity. He singled out Princess Jane di San Faustino as the most formidable creature on the Lido, a living advertisement for a new and increasingly fashionable type of marriage: that of American wealth to ancient but cash-strapped Italian breeding. According to Mosley, she was as witty as Emerald Cunard but less of a prude—though the standards by which he judged such things were demonstrably more flexible than those of most of his contemporaries. The princess had a strident

31   See Anne de Courcy's biography of Diana Mosley for a full account of these and other antics on the Lido.

American accent, though her statuesque appearance as described by Mosley was sufficient to prevent any but the most intrepid from venturing criticism. She wore white mourning, surely the ultimate in *chic de plage*, resembling a Roman matron as she stood daily on the beach in the blazing heat of July and August. Following an unwritten but widely acknowledged tradition, newcomers to the social scene presented themselves for inspection over tea in her *capanna*[32]. If she liked them, they were rewarded with smiles and a volley of New York pleasantry, refined by continental *savoir faire*. If not, then one was frozen out by what Mosley termed a 'basilisk' stare. He regarded this Lido campaign and her parties in Rome as constituting an ideal base-camp assault course for a young man aiming at dizzy social peaks: 'If he could stand up to the salon of Princess Jane, he could face much.' Mosley and Diana were divorced from Cimmie and Bryan before long. They turned their backs on adultery and were married in a discreet private ceremony in 1936, held in their friend Goebbels's drawing-room, with Hitler as the guest of honour.

32 Beach hut.

A FÜHRER ON THE FAIRWAY

The Golf Club at Alberoni—Il Circolo Golf Venezia as it is properly known—is one of the most charming and tranquil backwaters on the Lido, a good place for afternoon tea. The club house is an entertaining and eccentric amalgam of English, American and Italian style: ancient and unimpeachably shabby sofas and armchairs, cases of tarnished trophies, Ivy League-style honours boards, photos of regulars such as the Duke of Windsor, Bing Crosby and Henry Ford, a bar with an agreeably informal junior common room feel, and an acceptable quota of irascibly serious golfers, chic socialites, retreating men of letters and fragile A-list filmstars. The club was the brainchild of the motor-car magnate Henry Ford, who was mystified that a civilised city like Venice should have survived for so long without a golf course. Ford approached the ever enthusiastic Volpi and the two men set about finding a suitable site. The 100 hectares of lush, well planted and irrigated land around the old fort of Alberoni seemed an ideal spot. The best golf architects in the world, then Cruikshank of Glasgow, were commissioned to lay out nine compact but agreeably challenging holes (there are eighteen today).

The most notorious of the club's guests in its early days was Adolf Hitler, who visited the Lido in 1934 on

a state visit to Mussolini. Though Hitler's visit bore little resemblance to the grave pageant and elaborately
staged ritual prepared for Henri III and other visiting
heads of state it was, nevertheless, a piece of theatre
and an embarrassing one at that. The two most illu-
minating accounts are those by H.R. Knickerbocker[33],
the American foreign correspondent, and Elisabetta
Cerruti[34], wife of the Italian Ambassador to Germany.
Knickerbocker and his journalist colleagues stood in
an orderly line at the airfield, awaiting the arrival of
Hitler's Junkers. Mussolini was well prepared, dressed
in a general's uniform, a potent confection comprising
mirror-polished jackboots, crisp black shirt and imperi-
ally glistening gold braid. There was a spring to his step
and a detachment of beautifully dressed infantry lined
up beside him as a guard of honour. As Knickerbocker
pointed out, Mussolini was nothing if not a clever 'stage
manager', purposely arranging a Lido arrival to keep the
crowds at bay and Hitler suitably marginalised. Not for
the first time in its history, the Lido was to prove, in
Knickerbocker's words, 'a perfectly appointed theatre'.
When Hitler stepped out of the plane the contrast between the two men was dramatic, unnerving. Hitler's

33 Hubert Renfro Knickerbocker (1898–1949) was an American writer
and journalist, nicknamed 'Red' Knickerbocker from the colour of his hair,
He reported regularly for *Time* and other magazines in Europe and the USA
and won the Pulitzer Prize for his journalism.
34 Her memoirs, *Ambassador's Wife*, offer fascinating glimpses into life under Mussolini.

aide-de-camp, Konstantin von Neurath, had advised the Führer to wear civilian clothes, a correct and old-school prescription but scarcely a very astute one in view of Mussolini's formidable and by now widely publicised wardrobe. Hitler wore a shabby raincoat of English cut and an incongruously brand-new fedora. 'Beneath the obligatory cordiality,' says Knickerbocker, 'I could see an expression of amusement in Mussolini's eyes and of resentment in Hitler's.'

Hitler was swiftly transported to the Grand Hotel on the Grand Canal where, *Time* magazine tells us, the 'pantherlike Secretary of the Party, Achille Starace, and 80 bulging German detectives' shook the building with 'the tramp, tramp of their arrival'. Once safely behind the closed doors of his suite, Hitler hit the roof, raving at his staff, in particular at von Neurath, for allowing him to make such a fool of himself. The Grand, meanwhile, had spared no trouble to make his stay as comfortable as possible. Attention to detail was paramount and the hotel's Jewish pastry chef, one of the best in Venice, had been exiled to the Lido—to the Excelsior—for fear that his ethnicity (rather than his pastries) might cause offence.

There followed an unpleasant and mosquito-plagued meeting at the Villa Pisani in Stra, some miles inland on the Brenta Canal, followed by a twenty-five course dinner at which Hitler ostentatiously ate and drank nothing but vegetables and water. Mussolini walked

out halfway through, it was said from boredom. The
following day the leaders met again, this time at the
Golf Club, in order to discuss their respective intentions
for the future of Austria. They came to what historians
have sometimes described as a 'gentlemen's agreement',
on the face of it an appropriate outcome, given the
genteel setting. Germany for her part would hold back,
despite Hitler's avowed eagerness for Anschluss. Italy
too would hold back, recognising Austria's independence in spite of her own leanings towards territorial expansion. The body language between the two men was
embarrassing to watch. Hitler and Mussolini sat side
by side on a bench out on the fairway, some distance
from their aides. Hitler talked incessantly, gesticulat-
ing wildly and, according to Mussolini, quoting long
chunks of *Mein Kampf*. The eventual press conference
yielded little more than a single gem from Mussolini,
who announced that Germany and Italy were united
in a desire for what he termed a *pace virile*, a 'Virile
Peace'[35]. The luncheon afterwards, held at the club,
proved to be the most gruelling endurance test to date.
Elisabetta Cerruti reports that the cream of Venetian
society had been assembled for the occasion, many
of them very elderly and therefore drooping with ex-

---

35   The words he used were: 'Siamo diventati un popolo forte. La nostra
pace e quindi una pace virile, poiche la pace schiva i deboli e si accompagna
ai forti': 'We're a strong people. Our peace is therefore a virile peace. For
peace shuns the weak and cleaves to the strong.'

haustion in the heat. The food was inedible, the coffee undrinkable largely because, explains Signora Cerruti, the exiled Jewish pastry chef had been put in charge of the catering. Incensed at his exile to the Lido, he had spiked the coffee with salt. Neither Hitler nor Mussolini played golf, though had they done so the legendary par three ninth hole at Alberoni might well have served to dampen any vaunting military ambitions, since its major hazard is the old 18th-century fort of Alberoni, standing squarely between tee and green, with the added inconvenience of a moat.

HOUSES OF THE LIVING

During the Nazi occupation of Venice in 1943, the Herman Goering Military Band regularly performed Strauss and Bach in Piazza San Marco. Reporting on the Lido, the *Gazzettino* took a robustly pro-Nazi line. Venice was glad to be rid of the British with their 'angular skeletons, half-French hair-dos and make-up' and 'their vulgar horsey laughs from mouths much worked over with the gold of London dentistry'—not to mention their 'pet dogs', and their 'arrogance', coming over here and acting like *padroni* simply because they'd done Venice the 'honour' of exporting Byron, Browning and 'Ruskyn'. It was good to see the back of the French too, all those 'loafers' and 'false barons'. The press was quick to stamp on rumours, allegedly spread by 'Jews and Freemasons', that a date had been set for the closure of all the hotels, a measure that would have been disastrous for Venice. There were far fewer tourists on the Lido, claimed the *Gazzettino*, noting with disapproval that such young girls as could be seen wandering back from the beach were talking disconsolately about Byron and Schopenhauer rather than engaging, as would be proper, in wholesome, animated chatter about boys. Arrigo Cipriani recalled how his father was forced to put up a sign outside Harry's Bar saying 'Jews Not Welcome'. It was nonchalantly torn down on the same day by a Jewish regular who happened to pass by. Despite Harry's having been requisitioned as a mess hall for Mussolini's navy, Cipriani showed a robust disregard for authority, inviting many of his long-standing customers, some of them Jews and all of them good friends, to dine in the privacy of his home. At the beginning of the Nazi occupation, there were about 1,200 Jews in residence, but by August 1944, 205 of them had been deported to death camps, including the Chief Rabbi, Adolfo Ottolenghi.

The Jews had always encountered difficulties in Venice. Though the grant of the cemetery on the Lido in 1386[36] was an important symbolic gesture of acceptance and tolerance at the time, the fortunes of the community waxed and waned according to whatever commercial or political forces prevailed throughout Europe. Venetian anti-Semitism, a very real phenomenon, was born of two specific fears. First, there had been a widespread belief in the 16th century that Venetian Jews were conspiring with the Ottoman Turks to undermine Venetian supremacy in the Mediterranean.

---

36   The Benedictine friars of San Nicolò unsuccessfully sued the rabbi for the return of the land, even though the grant had been made by the Signoria, the ruling council of Venice, which was fully entitled to convey the land to whomever it wished. After much acrimony—the friars thought nothing of desecrating the Jewish graves under cover of darkness—the two communities became friendly neighbours. Honour was satisfied by the payment of a symbolic annual tribute by the rabbi to the abbot that included, among other items, a capon.

Secondly, since the Venetians were themselves an aggressively mercantile nation, they viewed with unease the increasingly prosperous community of Jewish moneylenders and merchants that had taken root in Venice from the early 13th century onwards. Whilst the Jews stimulated the economy—a welcome stimulus after expensive wars such as the one with Padua—it was nevertheless felt they should not be allowed to take too firm a root. Geographically, they were segregated first on the mainland, at Mestre, and then in the ghetto at Canareggio. In a ruling that foreshadowed Nazi oppression, they were forced to wear (though this ruling was not confined to Venice) distinguishing items of clothing: in 1394, a yellow badge; in 1496, a yellow hat; in 1500, a red hat. And there emerged every so often a scapegoat, a Jew whose activities were presented as being fatally prejudicial to Venetian interests. One such was Don Joseph Nasi, a Portuguese merchant who had set up at the Turkish court, building a massive trading empire that stretched from Antwerp to Palestine, completely bypassing the Venetian ports of the Mediterranean. Not only was 'Joseph the Jew' in league with the Turk, he was also, it was felt, gnawing away at the very guts of Venetian enterprise. These and many other tribulations ensured that Venetian Jews were consistently harried down the years. It is a pleasing irony that Daniele Manin, the hero of the Venetian uprising against Austria, was himself a Jew, albeit a Christian convert. He was, appropriately enough, the godson of the last doge, Lodovico Manin, from whom his family, originally the Fonsecas, had taken their new name upon conversion.

There are two Jewish cemeteries on the Lido. The ancient cemetery, founded in 1386, is on the Riviera San Nicolò. The modern, with memorials dating from the 17th century, is nearby on Via Cipro. While the modern cemetery is open to the public, the ancient may only be viewed by appointment and at a charge[37], though I was fortunate enough to be shown round—at no charge— by Aldo Izzo, a distinguished local historian, the custodian of the memorials and the energetic overseer of restoration. 'You're lucky,' said Leo, my Jewish friend, 'The last visitor he let in for nothing was Barbra Streisand.'

One of the most important monuments available for privileged inspection by me and Ms Streisand is that of Sara Copio Sullam, a formidable woman of letters and something of a yesteryear Yentl, in the sense that her thirst for Talmud scholarship was frowned on by the more orthodox members of the Jewish community as being inappropriate in a woman. Sullam was a leading figure in the 17th-century Venetian literary salon, the Sala degli Incognoscenti. Her epitaph celebrates her warmly as follows:

---

37   There are guided tours throughout the season and the funds raised are put towards the ongoing maintenance and restoration project, started in the 1990s. Benefactors include the Comune di Venezia, The Steven H. and Alida Brill Scheuer Foundation, The World Monument Fund and Venice in Peril.

This is the stone of the distinguished
Signora Sara
a woman of great genius,
wise among the wives,
supporter of the needy,
the unfortunate found in her a companion;
On the predestined day God will say:
come back, come back,
O Sulamita!

The 'Sulamita' is a pleasing play on her husband's name
Sullam, identifying Sara with the gorgeous Shulamite
in the *Song of Songs*. Her maiden name, Copio, means
'scorpion', hence the anatomically incorrect but decidedly venomous-looking creature at the head of the inscription, carved by the stonemason in open defiance of
the orthodox proscription in Deuteronomy 5:8, 'Thou
shalt not make thee any graven image, or any likeness
of any thing that is in heaven above, or that is in the
earth beneath, or that is in the waters beneath the earth.'

There are many such graven images in the Jewish
cemeteries—suns, moons, ladders, pitchers, trees of
life, the clasped hands of the high priest—all reminders
of how Jewish orthodoxy was eclipsed by the complex
international culture and symbolism of Jewish immi-
grants to Venice, keen to leave commemorations of their
trials and travels that were at least as vivid and attractive as those of their Christian counterparts. The lions

rampant to be found among the Jewish memorials here are neither lions of St Mark nor lions of Judah: they are lions of Castile and León, originally brought to Venice on the armorials of rich Sephardic warrior princes, expelled from Spain in 1492 by the Grand Inquisitor, Torquemada. The captivating deer peeping out of a basket is a symbol of the infant Moses; the proud woman standing at the top of a castellated tower, brandishing sword and palm branch, is the heroine of the Book of Proverbs, whose value is 'greater than rubies' and who 'laugheth at the time to come'; the intricate maze-like blazon seen on many of the stones is the *sigillum salomonis*, the Seal of Solomon, composed of a thread that has no end and that symbolises eternity; and the curious holes in the foot of some of the tablets represent the spectral corridors through which the souls of the departed find their way back to the remains of the body on the day of Resurrection.

The memorials in the ancient cemetery are neatly arranged in rows but still have a pleasing patina of moss, overgrown with the tendrils of wild flowers that Effie Ruskin would have seen and loved. In mid-morning, the sunlight dramatically illuminates the eastern reaches of the plot, animating the rescued pillars, tablets, steles and sarcophagi. The order introduced by Mr Izzo is a far cry from the chaos that prevailed in Byron's day and throughout the 19th century. The British painter Mortimer Luddington Menpes (1855–1938) observed that the graves were 'covered with sand and vegetation, and children never hesitate to dance on them—in fact, to do so is a favourite pastime. If one remonstrates, they will look at you with wide-open eyes, and explain that these are only graves of Jews—a Jew with the Venetians being no better than a dog. The grave of a Christian is treated with the greatest reverence: even the children and the gondoliers salute it as they pass. There is something pathetic about the Jewish graves, from the stones over which the inscriptions have been effaced.' John Addington Symonds, in his *Vagabunduli libellus*, captures something of the desolate charm of the neglected cemetery in those days:

> A tract of land swept by the salt sea foam,
> Fringed with acacia flowers, and billowy-deep
> In meadow grasses, where tall poppies sleep,
> And bees athirst for wilding honey roam.
> How many a bleeding heart hath found its home
> Under these hillocks which the sea-mews sweep!
> Here knelt an outcast race to curse and weep,
> Age after age, 'neath heaven's unanswering dome.
> Sad is the place, and solemn. Grave by grave,
> Lost in the dunes, with rank weeds overgrown,
> Pines in abandonment; as though unknown,
> Uncared for, lay the dead, whose records pave
> This path neglected; each forgotten stone
> Wept by no mourner but the moaning wave.

Yet despite the beauty of Symonds's pastoral vision, the present regime is undoubtedly preferable to the 'path neglected', especially since the work of Mr Izzo and others has enhanced rather than detracted from the natural beauty of the site. There is still a sufficient luxuriance of enchanted undergrowth and leafy canopy to enable visitors to conjure up the irregular or riotous happenings of the past: Lord Byron's irritation, as he dismounted here, at a gawping gaggle of young, female day trippers to the Lido; or George Sand, during one of the spectacular rows she frequently had with her lover, the poet Alfred de Musset, 'leaping from tombstone to tombstone' as he pursued her through the Adriatic dusk; or Horatio Brown at picnic with a carefree symposium of youthful gondoliers.

The 'modern' cemetery in Via Cipro is open to the public and is a fine place to walk, history having conveniently divided the House of the Living into a series of historical rooms, century by century, interlinked by paths shaded by palms and cypresses. Again, as in the ancient cemetery, the 17th, 18th and 19th-century sectors are full of monuments dramatically at variance with Jewish orthodoxy: there is intricately brocaded stonework commemorating families whose fortunes were founded on Burano lace; there are delightfully inappropriate Baroque *putti* upholding pillars and stonework symbolic of the Wailing Wall; the 19th century sees cavernous mausolea, massive spheres and obelisks and, in a final flourish of the liberal spirit, an intricate *cinerarium* with copper, marble and glass urns, curlicued wrought-iron tracery and a pediment-ed canopy overgrown with ivy. The 20th-century me-morials, by contrast, represent a return to orthodoxy. Though there are sobering memorials of the Holocaust here, there still arrive, every spring and summer, the living creatures that William Sharp[38] encountered in the 19th century: 'hundreds of butterflies, lizards, bees, birds, and some heavenly larks—a perfect glow and tumult of life.'

---

38   William Sharp (1855–1905) was a Scottish poet, biographer and edi-tor who also wrote as Fiona MacLeod, a pseudonym kept secret during his lifetime. He also edited the poetry of Ossian, Walter Scott, Matthew Arnold, Algernon Charles Swinburne and Eugene Lee-Hamilton.

ELEPHANTS & ECOSYSTEMS

There are plenty of natural and scientific wonders to be uncovered on the sands of the Lido. In times past it was much visited by the women of Venice, the respectable ones as much as the courtesans, and bathing on the Lido was the accepted equivalent of visiting the spas of today. The sand itself was used as a basis for facial scrubs and masks:

> The treatment of the skin was a speciality of the Venetian women. The use of the bath was one of their inheritances, they bathed the whole body frequently, sometimes in the sea at the Lido, but every house had its bath—in humble homes of wood or common metal, in patrician palaces of porcelain, glass, or silver. With the water they mixed simple or exotic perfumes. One of their secrets was to remain, with the whole body immersed and motionless, for at least half an hour; and another was, they never rubbed the skin but just dabbed it and let it dry naturally. Then the nostrums of the masseusses' art were exploited, A not uncommon custom was to lay a slice of raw veal, dipped in new milk, upon the face at night! For richer women other artifices followed suit—puffs and powders to gently temper the epidermis or hide

unsightly blotches, and pigments—rouge and others—with which art might most effectively colour crude or enervated nature. With respect to the recipes employed in the concoction of the tinctures little can be authoritatively said, for each fair one kept her elixir and its secret to herself. Anyhow, generally speaking, one may say that the finest of fine Lido golden sand, crushed vitreous plaques of Murano, ivory sawdust, pounded sea-shells and—in exuberant and extravagant humour—even powdered pearls, and precious gold dust were employed. Vegetable compounds—the juice of grapes, berberis, ivy-berries, lemon-squash and orange-flavour, with aromatic powders of all sorts and kinds were also used. Dyes, strictly so called, were not in favour: their effect was ephemeral.[39]

In an absorbing monograph entitled 'The Lido as Venice's refuse tip: Dalmatian sheep and the 1819 elephant', Professor Virgilio Giormani reminds us that before its ascendancy as a beach resort, the Lido had been put to pastoral and agricultural use, fertilised by a continuous supply of Venice's rubbish, 'scoasse', discarded food and waste from the vegetable markets. This rich source was further augmented by the dung of cattle and sheep,

39　*The Dogaressas of Venice: The Wifes of the Doges* by Edgcumbe Staley, 1845.

imported from Dalmatia and pastured on the Lido to
fatten them up for market after the rigours of their voyage. A significant spin-off of this enterprise was the discovery that sheep dung, if properly treated, could be
used in the production of saltpetre, an important in-
gredient of gunpowder and thus a valuable commodity.
Every effort was made to encourage and streamline the
process. The animals would be corralled in specially-
built stockades so that the dung could be concentrated
in one convenient place, scraped up and loaded into
sacks for processing. As for the elephant in Professor
Giormani's paper, it was, it seems, the largest and most
bizarre item ever transported to the Lido *scoasseria* for
disposal. This elephant, part of a circus act in the carnival of 1819, had escaped from its cage on the Riva degli
Schiavoni and ran amok in the streets of Venice. Pursued by the militia, it took refuge, angry and terrified,
in the nearby church of Sant'Antonin. After permission
had been granted by the Patriarch, a cannon was drawn
up outside the church, the doors thrown open and the
elephant blown to kingdom come. Byron wrote to Hobhouse on 17th May 1819: 'An Elephant went Mad here
about two months ago—killed his keeper—knocked
down a house—broke open a Church—dispersed all
his assailants and was at last killed by a Shot in his *pos-
teriore* from a field-piece brought from the Arse–nal on
purpose.' The remains were dumped on the Lido but
before long the skeleton was exhumed by a group of en-

terprising zoologists and reconstructed in the University of Padua. It would have come as no consolation to the elephant that in certain quarters he was thought not to have died in vain. The Venetian poet Pietro Buratti wrote an 800-verse poem on the episode, in dialect, entitled *Elefanteide: Storia Verissima dell'Elefante*. This satirical work was an attack on the Austrian government in which the elephant stood for the potent, virile and troublesome spirit of Venice, criminally emasculated by its foreign overlords. Buratti was sent to prison for a month for his pains.

George Ames Plimpton (1927–2003), the American journalist, author, editor and actor, had an unusually fortunate spell of war service, some of it in Venice. He arrived in Europe two weeks after the fighting ended and spent much of his time on the Lido where, as his British friend Sir Andrew Leggatt recalls, 'he had the stupefying good luck, even for George, to be assigned to teach social graces and military techniques' to his fellow conscripts. Plimpton had a good time, and remained unabashed at possible accusations that he might be dismissed as a fun-loving dilettante. He was convinced, he claimed, that there was nothing 'inherently wrong' in having fun. Plimpton taught public speaking outdoors, beneath a maple tree outside the walls of the barracks near San Nicolò. He was a keen birdwatcher but uncertain as to how this would sit with the US Army, assuming, in all probability correctly, that his brother officers might look slightly askance at any GI prone to lyricising the habits of the white-throated sparrow. Goats, cows and geese disrupted his class, but the worst distraction were the barn swallows, fearless creatures who would dive-bomb Plimpton's students and occasionally snatch an insect from a nose or ear[40].Plimpton would also have caught sight of many of the birds that live on or visit the Lido to this day: wintering Kentish plovers, dunlin, ringed plovers, black-throated divers. Housman too discovered a natural paradise on the northern reaches of the Lido: 'On this same island I also discovered a bit of real country; grass and a grove of trees round about the fort of St Nicolò, where the Venetians have their great picnic in May. In addition to the usual English autumn wildflowers there was purple salvia and the evening primrose. There were also very attractive grasshoppers two inches long, which they call by the name "salto-martino".' Professor Gerard H. Gurney, Fellow of the Entomological Society, memorably records[41] his quest for the elusive butterfly *Issoria lathonia*: 'A single rather worn male was caught close to the Excelsior Hotel.'

---

40   For the source of these anecdotes, see *George, Being George: George Plimpton's Life as Told, Admired, Deplored, and Envied by 200 Friends, Relatives, Lovers, Acquaintances, Rivals—and a Few Unappreciative Observers*. Nelson W. Aldrich.
41   In *The Entomologist*, Volume the Forty-Sixth. West, Newman & Co, London, 1913.

PRINCIPAL SIGHTS ON THE LIDO

Gran Viale Santa Maria Elisabetta

The Gran Viale is the main street of the Lido, running in a straight line from the vaporetto station to the beach. There is an agreeable and ever-increasing sense of expectation to be felt as, either Goethe-like or equipped simply with bucket and spade, one saunters towards the Adriatic. If you have no bucket and spade, the shops lining the street will be happy to provide them. There is a good mix of cafés and restaurants and every evening, in or out of season, there is a civilised parade of good-looking young Italians, grave elderly ladies and gentlemen, sedate spaniels and poodles and the occasional cat. The pleasing criss-cross of streets on either side of the Gran Viale are mainly residential, though some also contain further restaurants and shops.

Santa Maria della Vittoria, Il Tempio Votivo della Pace di Venezia

The Tempio Votivo, as it is commonly known, is Venice's war memorial. The imposing copper-domed structure, near to the vaporetto station, is the first thing most visitors to the Lido see and remember. Built by the architect Giuseppe Torres in 1935, it was commis-

sioned by the then Cardinal Patriarch of Venice, Pietro
la Fontaine. Cardinal la Fontaine had great affection
for the Lido, where he often spent quiet hours on the
beach walking in prayer and meditation.
Riviera Santa Maria Elisabetta 2.

San Nicolò al Lido and associated buildings

The church is open to the public and situated on the
Riviera San Nicolò. The main attraction, unjustly dismissed by Ruskin, are the exquisitely carved walnut
choir stalls made in 1636 by Giovanni da Crema and
Camillo di San Luca. The panels depict 27 scenes from
the life of St Nicholas. A Baroque polychrome marble
altar contains his remains and those of St Theodore.
Though the building was extensively remodelled in the
post-Palladian building flurry of the 18th century, it
preserves important Corinthian columns and capitals.
There is also an austere 14th-century life-size carved
wooden crucifix. The earliest building of note on the
Lido is the former **Benedictine monastery at San
Nicolò**, founded in the 11th century, now a study cen-
tre. The 16th-century Renaissance cloisters are beautiful—they stood in for a Brazilian monastery in the
James Bond film *Moonraker*. Nearby is the **Palazzetto
del Consiglio dei Dieci**, c. 1520. The 16th-century
bridge on the Riviera San Nicolò is made of brick and
Istrian stone and is now a key stage in the annual marriage with the sea, at which the mayor of Venice stands

in for the doge in an enjoyable ceremony, albeit considerably toned down since the days of the original *sposalizio* (*see p. 18*).

Other churches on the Lido

Sant'Antonio was built in 1936 for the local congregation as a sturdier alternative to the makeshift tent on the beach where they had worshipped until then. It is a light, airy building in an eclectic Veneto-Byzantine style, though its simplicity also invokes Rationalist principles. The church of **Santa Maria Elisabetta** near the vaporetto station was built in the mid-16th century as an oratory and converted into a church in 1627. There is an interesting font with bronze representations of the four Evangelists on its cover, the face of St Mark having striking leonine characteristics. **Santa Maria Nascente** is a small church attached to the former **Ospedale al Mare**, an important site currently being transformed into a residential resort. Built in 1932, the church is decorated with paintings by Giuseppe Cherubini, who also decorated the Teatrino Liberty (*see p. 142*). **Santa Maria Assunta** in the Piazza Maggiore at Malamocco dates from the 12th century and contains memorials to the settlement's original ruling family, the Pisani. There is an intriguing Baroque painting, *Il selvataggio miracoloso* by Girolamo Forabosco, commemorating the rescue from a shipwreck of the artist's patron, Giovanni Ventura. The drenched but fashionably-dressed figures strike noble attitudes on the shore. Also of note is a chilling work depicting the exorcism of St Mary Magdalene.

The Jewish Cemeteries

The cemeteries are described in detail on p. 122. The old cemetery at the corner of Riviera San Nicolò and Via Cipro may be viewed by appointment, while the new cemetery is open to the public daily, closing only on the 25th December, 1st January and 1st May. Further details of opening times and ongoing restoration projects can be seen at www.museoebraico.it.

The Catholic Cemetery

The Catholic Cemetery is in Via Cipro, between the two Jewish cemeteries. Like the new Jewish cemetery, it is open to the public and a pleasant place to visit. In one sector there are memorials rescued from the Protestant Cemetery that was obliterated in the 1930s during the expansion of the Aeroporto Nicelli. Rescued tombstones include that of John Murray the art dealer, and the temperamental English soprano Catherine Tofts (c. 1685–1756). Her husband, Joseph Smith (1682–1770), the British Consul in Venice, was also buried here but his memorial has been removed to St George's, the Anglican church in Dorsoduro. Smith presented Goethe with a copy of Palladio's *Quattro Libri*, a gift which touched the German poet, who visited Smith's grave on the Lido in the 1780s to offer a prayer of thanks.

Aeroporto Nicelli

Aeroporto Nicelli (*see p. 98*) is the headquarters of the Aeroclub Ancillotto, the flying club of Venice. You may land helicopters and private light aircraft here by prior arrangement. A charter company offers sightseeing flights of varying durations and, thankfully as a separate package, tuition in *paracadutismo*, parachuting. The airport has become a well-known venue for concerts and lectures and the public spaces can be hired for parties or conferences. There is a popular restaurant and bar. The Nicelli website (www.aeroportonicelli.it) gives an interesting overview of the airport's history.
Riviera San Nicolò 1, T: 041 526 0808.

20th-Century Architecture: the 'Liberty' Villas

The principal buildings of interest are described in the chapter 'Venal Moonshine', though there are hundreds of examples to be seen when walking on the Lido. The Comune di Venezia has published a useful and ever-expanding online list of important buildings on the Lido, with maps, photographs and plans together with biographies of the architects, designers and patrons. The site (www2.comune.venezia.it/lidoliberty) is of enormous use to those planning 'Liberty' walking tours of the Lido. Most structures listed, with the exception of the hotels and civic buildings, are closed to the public, though their façades and gardens are for the most part easily visible from the street. Doors, gateways, cornices, even bell-plates and post-boxes, are often textbook examples of Art Deco and Art Nouveau styling. 'Liberty' is the wholly inadequate catch-all term used in Italy to describe the hotels and villas built by architects and their patrons from the beginning of the 20th century. Owing little if anything to the influential English designer Arthur Lasenby Liberty, from whom the name is taken, they are exuberant fusions of a great many styles: northern European Art Deco, Veneto-Byzantine-Moorish revivalism, Rationalism humorously tempered by Art Nouveau flourishes. There are, on the Lido, curiosities that elude classification. One such is a hotel, the Albergo alle Quattro Fontane at Via Quattro Fontane 16, a pleasing extravaganza that recalls a Swiss alpine chalet but has touches of Viennese Secessionist refinement.

Circolo Golf Venezia: the Alberoni Golf Club

This is Venice's 18-hole golf course, its site protected by the World Wildlife Fund. See p. 114 and the club website, www.circologolfvenezia.it.

Pineta degli Alberoni

The ancient pine forests of Alberoni are at the southernmost tip of the Lido, accessible by bus or bicycle travelling along the western shore of the Lido via Malamocco. Alternatively, another way is to walk or cycle along the *murazzi* (*see p. 16*) and approach the pine forest from the Spiaggia Alberoni (Bagni Alberoni), the wild beach whose dunes blend gradually into the depths of the forest. Out of season, in February and early March, the forest is practically deserted save for a few birdwatchers, dog walkers, poets and painters. These are the enchanted far reaches of the Lido where Byron, Goethe and Chateaubriand loved to ride and walk. The charm of the desolate location seems all the more precious, it has to be said, for its proximity to Venice, incredibly only twenty minutes away. In high season the forest and beach can become rather more lively. There is a gay presence, and at the height of July entire volleyball teams of Tadzios caper about in the dunes and shallows.

Blue Moon

This extraordinary beach complex off Piazzale Bucintoro at the end of the Gran Viale was designed and built by Giancarlo de Carlo in 1999. His proposal was the winning entry in a competition organised by the Comune di Venezia in response to increasing concern that the once-glamorous Lido had become shabby, sordid and run-down. It is an important building because though it is over ten years old, it marks the beginning of the latest wave of regeneration on the Lido. Like the best of Lido architecture, it defies easy classification, being an extravagant fantasy structure that would not look out of place in a Fellini film. Indeed, the name Blue Moon was borrowed from a glamorous nightclub that had existed on this spot in the 1950s and had been the haunt of a

local and international set committed to the pursuit of
the *dolce vita*. Blue Moon has public spaces for music,
dancing, films, live theatre and concerts. There are intimate areas better suited to flirting, playing cards, intel-
lectual discussion or wistful contemplation. The Blue
Moon serves the Spiaggia Comunale, the public beach
at the northernmost end of the Lido. Though this beach
is by no means as picturesque as its counterpart at Alberoni (*see above*), the shoreline becomes wilder and
more desolate the further north one walks, the revelry
of the Blue Moon soon becoming little more than a distant glitter and buzz in the gathering twilight.

The Lion's Bar
Diagonally opposite the Excelsior on Lungomare
Guglielmo Marconi, the Lion's is a favourite resort of
journalists and photographers during the Film Festival.
The façade of the corner entrance is an elaborate affair,
designed by Giovanni Sicher in the 1920s, featuring a
vast sky-blue and gold sunburst demilune. I visited the
Lion's out of season one early evening. There was nobody about but a dazed-looking barefoot blonde, pos-
sibly the ghost of a Fellini extra, swaying slowly back
and forth in the inner room under a massive glitterball.
The bar is as much frequented by arty types as by journalists, and the Felliniesque *danseuse* is a fair indication
of the agreeable, if somewhat eccentric, atmosphere one
might encounter here.

Biblioteca Hugo Pratt

The public library of the Lido is housed in the former Malamocco home of the Venetian artist Hugo Eugenio Pratt (1927–95) who was best known for his graphic novels featuring the character Corto Maltese, an enigmatic sailor-adventurer. The reading rooms are pleasant and there are frequent art exhibitions and talks.
Via Sandro Gallo 136, T: 041 526 8991.

The Planetarium

The sixty-seat Venice Planetarium (Planetario di Venezia) is third largest planetary dome in Italy, open to the public as well as being the venue for lectures and gatherings of the Amateur Astronomers Association of Venice.
Lungomare d'Annunzio, area ex Luna Park. Open on Sun Oct–May, www.astrovenezia.net.

The Museum of Malamocco

The collection is housed in the Palazzo del Podestà, a 15th-century Gothic building in Piazza Maggiore, opposite the church of Santa Maria Assunta. The palace itself is of interest, with a fine mullioned window and, on the elevation facing the church, a triple lancet window with two bas-reliefs, on the right a lion and on the left a deer bearing a shield, the emblem of Malamocco. There is a permanent exhibition devoted to the history of Malamocco from its earliest days. Photographic storyboards and artefacts document the arrival of settlers from the mainland, the growth of Malamocco as a seat of government and the eventual desertion of the settlement in favour of the high ground of Rialto, now Venice proper. In 1107 Malamocco was completely destroyed by an earthquake that swept away the promontory and harbour around which it was built. A new community emerged and over the centuries Malamocco built up a quiet and uninterrupted prosperity as a fishing village. *Palazzo del Podestà, Piazza Maggiore, Malamocco, T: 041 272 0560.*

The Teatrino Liberty

At the time of writing, this exquisite theatre was being restored as part of the transformation of the former Ospedale al Mare. Originally built in the 1930s for the entertainment of patients at the hospital, it fell into disrepair after the Second World War and was until recently used as a junk room to store archive boxes and unwanted furniture. There are lively frescoes by Giuseppe Cherubini and an enormous Lion of St Mark in Art Deco stained glass. Details of the restoration project are covered in full at www.estuarionostro.org/teatrino-liberty.php.

SIGHTS OF INTEREST
NEAR THE LIDO

The Museum of Pellestrina

The museum at Pellestrina, south of the Lido, comple-
ments that of Malamocco, explaining in depth some of
the challenges that were faced by early settlers in the
lagoon and which still exercise the Venetian authorities
today, in particular sea erosion and floods in the lagoon.
The two principal exhibits explore the history of the
murazzi (*see p. 16*) and give an account of the floods
of 1966. Future projects include exhibitions devoted to
fishing, shipbuilding, lace, the Venetian dialect, textiles
and cooking.

*Piccolo Museo della Laguna, sud S. Pietro in Volta—ex
Scuola Goldoni, T: 333 614 3976.*

Forte di Sant'Andrea

The Forte di Sant'Andrea is easily reached from the
Lido. Also known as Castelnuovo, it was built in 1543
by Michele Sanmicheli. An external bastion surrounds
the central stronghold. There is a plaque on the tower
commemorating the Battle of Lepanto and a terrace at
the summit affords a spectacular view of Venice. On
April 20th, 1797, the commander of the fort ordered
his garrison to open fire on the French warship, *La*

Libérateur d'Italie, as it sailed into the lagoon. Napoleon retaliated by marching on Venice. The doge, Lodovico Manin, surrendered and this marked the end of the Republic. The fort can be visited by appointment.
Isola di Sant'Andrea (Le Vignole), T: 041 241 3717.

San Lazzaro degli Armeni
The island is the home of the Armenian monastery of the Mekhitarist Order. There is a permanent exhibition devoted to Byron, who studied Armenian here during his time in Venice and assisted the fathers with the preparation of an Armenian Grammar. The garden is noted for its peacocks. The island may be reached by vaporetto and there are guided tours by arrangement with the Fathers.

SERVICES & FACILITIES ON THE LIDO

TRANSPORT

Vaporetti: Numbers 1 and 2 leave from Piazzale S.M. Elisabetta and connect the Lido to San Marco and the Giudecca. Numbers 51 and 52 skirt the northern perimeter of Venice via S. Pietro in Castello and Fondamente Nuove.

Alilaguna: The Alilaguna waterbus service leaves from Piazzale S.M. Elisabetta every half hour and connects the Lido to Marco Polo airport.

Buses: Regular buses run north to south, the length of the Lido from San Nicolò to Alberoni via the Gran Viale. A ferry service runs from Alberoni to Pellestrina, subsequently connecting with bus and boat services running as far as Chioggia.

Cars: The car ferry leaves from Riviera San Nicolò, near Via Cipro, and plies to and fro from Venice and Punta Sabbioni.

Bicycle hire: Gardin Anna Vallì: Piazzale S.M. Elisabetta, T: 041 276 0005; **Lido on Bike:** Gran Viale 21, T: 041 526 8019.

BEACHES

Aurora Beach Club: Lungomare d'Annunzio 20, T: 041 526813.

Bagni Alberoni: Strada Nuova dei Bagni 26, T: 041 731029.

Blue Moon: Piazzale Bucintoro 1, T: 041 526 0236.

Consorzio Alberghi e Pensioni Lido (CAPLI): Lungomare Marconi 22, T: 041 526 0356.

Kuyaba: Lungomare Marconi 85, T: 041 526 5961.

Miramare: Lungomare Marconi 61/c, T: 041 526 0193.

Paradise Beach (Spiaggia Paradiso): Via Spiaggia Libera San Nicolò (Viale Klinger), T: 041 526 0303.

Spiaggia Caribe: Lungomare Marconi 58.

Spiaggia des Bains, Spiaggia Excelsior/Amaranti: (Il Reef Bar, snacks; Beach Pagoda and Beach Rotonda Lounge, cheap meals), Uffici SAB (Stabilimenti Attività Balneari), Lungomare Marconi 34–36, T: 041 271 6808.

Stabilimento Balneare Sorriso: Via Colombo 22.

Venezia Spiagge: Lungomare d'Annunzio, T: 041 526 0236.

Venezia Spiagge: Piazzale Ravà, T: 041 526 1249.

CAMPING

Camping San Nicolò: Via dei Sanmicheli 14, T: 041 526 7415, www.campingsannicolo.com.

SPORT

General Sportcenter Lido: Via Antoniotto Usodimare, T: 041 526 9450.

Fishing

Unione Sportiva Lido Pesca: Via Malamocco 16, T: 041 770420.

Fitness

Planet Dance n' Fitness:

Lungomare Marconi 52/a,
T: 041 242 0488.

Golf

Circolo Golf Venezia: Via del Forte Alberoni, T: 041 731333.

Riding

Circolo Ippico Veneziano: Via Colombo 1, T: 041 526 5162.

Rollerskating

Pattinaggio: A.S. Venezia Roller Club, Pattinodromo Quattro Fontane, Via Falier, T: 041 526 0382.

Shooting

Poligono di Tiro a Segno Nazionale Sezione di Venezia: Riviera San Nicolò 23, T: 041 526 0127.

Subaqua

Freetime S.r.l.: Diving Center e Scuola di Sub, Gran Viale 3, T: 348 260 5616.

Tennis

Club Cà del Moro: c/o Centro Sportivo Cà del Moro, Via Ferruccio Parri 6, T: 041 770801.

RESTAURANTS

Trattoria La Favorita: Via Francesco Duodo 33.
Trattoria La Battigia: Via Nicosia 14.
Ristorante Al Passator Cortese: Via Lepanto 8.
Ristorante La Tavernetta:
Via Francesco Morosini 4.
Bar Pizzeria Da Tiziano: Via Sandro Gallo 96/a.
Trattoria Al Ponte Di Borgo: Rio Terà, Malamocco.

SUPERMARKETS

Central Lido: Coop. Adriatica, Via G. Fuga 12.
North Lido: Coop. Adriatica, Via Marco Polo 19.

Billa, Gran Viale, at the top, near the lagoon end.

CHEMISTS

Alla Marina: Via Malamocco 2/a, T: 041 770128.

Baldisserotto: Gran Viale 55/a, T: 041 526 0117.

Città Giardino: Via Sandro Gallo 112/b, T: 041 526 1130.

Ca' Bianca: Via Sandro Gallo 211, T: 041 526 7251.

Excelsior: Via Sandro Gallo 74, T: 041 526 1587.

Schlecker: Gran Viale 79 (on the left as you walk towards the sea).

INDEX

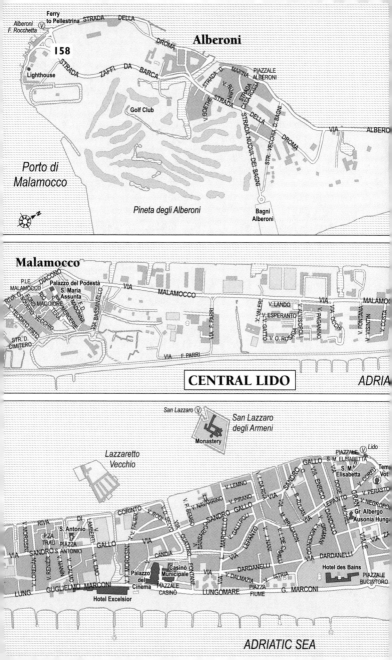

Alberoni

Ferry to Pellestrina
Alberoni F. Rocchetta
STRADA DELLA
DROMA
158
Lighthouse
STRADA
ZAFFI DA BARCA
V. GOETHE
STRADA D
STRADA
V. RUFFINI
MARINA
PIAZZALE ALBERONI
STRADA C. SA ROSSA
STRADA C. DEI BAGNI
STRADA DELLA DROMA
STR. VECCHIA DEI BAGNI
STRADA NUOVA DEI BAGNI
VIA
ALBERO

Golf Club

Porto di Malamocco

Pineta degli Alberoni

Bagni Alberoni

Malamocco

P.LE MALAMOCCO
DIACOMO
RIVA GREGORIO
FONDO PRIOLI
FEUDITO IPATO
VECCHIO
STR. D. CIMITERO
Palazzo del Podestà
S. Maria Assunta
MERCERIE
VIA E.D.
MAGGIORE
VIA BASSANELLO
VIA MALAMOCCO
VIA F. PARRI
VIA F. PARRI
V. LANDO
V. VALERI
V. ESPERANTO
V. PAGANINO
V. GIUSTINIANI
V. CUSTODI
V.O. ROSI
VIA FONTANA
VIA OCCHI
V. VISINTIN
V. COSTA
VIA MALAMO

CENTRAL LIDO

ADRIA

San Lazzaro Ⓥ
San Lazzaro degli Armeni
Monastery

Lazzaretto Vecchio

PIAZZALE
S. M. ELISABETTA
S. M. Elisabetta
Tem
Vot
Ⓥ Lido
V. GALLO
VIALE ENRICO
VIA CORFU
Gr. Albergo Ausonia Hungaria
V. NEGROPONTE
V. PERASTO
V. MOROSINI
V. LORENZO
RIVA DI
LAMBERTI
S. Antonio
P.ZA TRAU
PIAZZA S. ANTONIO
V. RENIER
V. MANN
V. CLLIO
V. ELBO
V. DANDOLO
CORINTO
V. FILERI
V. ROD. SESTO
VIA
CANDIA
V. LEMNO
V. NAVARRINO
V. P. BEMBO
V. PIRANO
V. DA RIVA
SANDRO GALLO
BARBARO
MARCELLO
LEPANTO
V. GALLIPOLI
V. ZUZIN
V. P. ZULIAN
V. BRAGADIN
V. DE PRETI
V. MICHIEL
V. DOGE
V. GRIMANI
DOMENICO
VIALE
VIA
DARDANELLI
Hotel des Bains
GUGLIELMO MARCONI
Hotel Excelsior
Palazzo del Cinema
Casinò Municipale
PIAZZALE CASINÒ
V. FONTANE
V. DALMAZIA
V. DARDANELLI
V. ISTRIA
PIAZZA FIUME
LUNGOMARE
G. MARCONI
PIAZZALE BUCINTORO
LUNG.
SANDRO

ADRIATIC SEA

VENETIAN LAGOON

Malamocco

P. del Podestà
S. Maria
Assunta
S. Maria
MAGGIORE

VIA ALBERONI
VIA ALBERONI
RIVA G. DIEDO
DOGE BEATO
FOND. DI BORGO
FOND. S. SPERO VECCHIO
CALLE FERA
RIO TERA
MERCERIE

V. DOGE GALLA
V. D. G. GALBAIO
DOGE ORSEOLO
DOGE GRADENIGO
STR. D. CIMITERO

ADRIATIC SEA

0 ___ 500 yards
0 ___ 500 metres

VENETIAN LAGOON

Lido

Lazzaretto
Vecchio

PASQUALI
RIVA
GIOVANNI E VINDELINO DA SPIRA
RIVIERA B. MARCELLO
RIVA
DI
CORINTO
ALBRIZZI
F. GATTI
F. PETRARCA
VIA NICOLA JANSON
V. LONGHENA
V. VIVALDI
V. CANALETTO
V. LOREDAN MOROSINI
S. Antonio
LAMBERTI
AINE
V. TASSO
SANDRO
V. DASSA
V. F. LEGA
GALLO
Biblioteca
Pratt
P.LE
F. GRIMANI
VIA
V. LOREDAN
SANDRO
P.ZA TRAÙ
PIAZZA
S. ANTONIO
GALLO
V. HERTZ
V. D. KIRCHMAYR
VIA A. USODIMARE
VIA
V. DE MAO
VIA COLOMBO
MEDUSE
LUNGOMARE
GUGLIELMO
MARCONI

Hotel Excelsior

A

0 ___ 500 yards
0 ___ 500 metres

VENETIAN LAGOON

Porto
di
Lido

o

Ferry
Lido - S. Nicolò
P.LE
SAN NICOLÒ
SAN NICOLÒ
RIVIERA SAN NICOLÒ
V. XMII
SANMICHELI
ITTA
RIVIERA
DUODO
V. CIPRO
SAN NICOLÒ
VIA MARCO
Old Jewish
Cemetery
San Nicolò
al Lido
V. MOREA
Catholic
Cemetery
P.
G. NICELLI
V. MORO
IO
V. CIPRO
VIA CIPRO
New Jewish
Cemetery
VIA G. SELVA
VIA POLO
ARENZO
ZZA
LA
D'ANNUNZIO
STR. D. L'OSPIZIO MARINO
Ospedale
al Mare
PIAZZALE
RAVÀ
Aeroporto Nicelli
VIALE UMBERTO KLINGER
Spiaggia
Comunale

0 ___ 500 yards
0 ___ 500 metres

The Venice Lido: A Blue Guide Travel Monograph
First edition 2011.

Published by Blue Guides Limited, a Somerset Books Company
Winchester House, Deane Gate Avenue, Taunton, Somerset TA1 2UH
www.blueguides.com. 'Blue Guide' is a registered trade mark.

Cover design by Hadley Kincade.
Cover image: 'Au Lido', from the album *Le Bonheur du Jour*,
by George Barbier, 1924, courtesy of The Art Archive/
Kharbine-Tapabor/Coll. Galdoc-Grob.
Back cover: The Hotel Excelsior and its beach,
photo by Thomas Howells.

Maps by Dimap Bt.
Design and typesetting by Anikó Kuzmich, Blue Guides.

A CIP catalogue record of this book is available from the British Library.

Distributed in the United States of America by WW Norton and
Company, Inc. of 500 Fifth Avenue, New York, NY 10110.

ISBN 978-1-905131-50-1

Printed and bound in Hungary by Pauker Nyomdaipari Kft.